The Island from Within

*A COMPOSITE PORTRAIT OF
THE ISLE OF WIGHT*

edited by Roger Sawyer

To Pat and Moskie

Contents

Foreword: CLIFF MICHELMORE *Page 6*

Preface *Page 8*

Acknowledgements *Page 8*

Contributors *Page 11*

Carisbrooke Castle: JACK JONES *Page 13*

Royalty and the Isle of Wight: SARAH PIGOT *Page 17*

The High Sheriff of the Isle of Wight: DENYS PEEL *Page 22*

Nunwell - The Softer Touch: TONY AYLMER *Page 27*

Queen Victoria and Osborne: KAY McDONALD *Page 32*

Newtown: PATRICIA SIBLEY *Page 38*

The Worsley Monument - Brading Sea-Mark - Bronze Age Remains: ROBERT POMEROY *Page 41*

Bembridge Sailing Club: ROBIN COLVILLE *Page 43*

Centurion's Copse: JAMES COLVILLE *Page 44*

Overners - An Anthropological Survey: REGGIE BENNETT *Page 47*

J. Howard Whitehouse and the Ruskin Galleries at Bembridge School: JAMES S. DEARDEN *Page 50*

Literary Connections with the Isle of Wight: HUGH NOYES *Page 55*

Some Painters of the Isle of Wight: PAMELA FREEMAN *Page 60*

The Fort and its Walk: ROGER SAWYER *Page 62*

The Victorian Fortifications of the Isle of Wight: ANTHONY CANTWELL AND PETER SPRACK *Page 65*

The Island in the Second World War: BILL CURLING *Page 69*

The Isle of Wight Hunt: MICHAEL POLAND *Page 73*

The Isle of Wight Foot Beagles: PHILIP MITCHESON *Page 77*

Yacht Clubs and Yachting in the Isle of Wight: HARRY CHILLINGWORTH *Page 79*

Royal Corinthian YC: ROBIN COLVILLE *Page 82*

In Pursuit of Natural History: OLIVER H. FRAZER *Page 83*

The Railways of the Isle of Wight: ALAN DOE *Page 88*

Quarr Abbey: DENIS BRADLEY *Page 91*

Foreword
CLIFF MICHELMORE

In the days before all-night ferries those of us born on the Isle of Wight came to realize how very fortunate we were and how unfortunate the 'Overners' were. As the last paddle boat moored at Fountain Pier and Fairy the barman/steward made his way to the nearest pub, we knew that we were in a place apart. We could look across the Solent at the mainland and see the strings of lights along the sea fronts which would gradually go out.

There was no putting out of the light from Egypt Point which warned sailors where they were: Cowes, that was where they were. There is no doubt that islanders the world over feel that they are in some ways different from mainlanders because the sea is all around them. At any rate I felt different and I still do whenever I cross that narrow stretch of water. It is not isolation but separation and being apart.

Boyhood in Cowes after the First World War meant the revival of Cowes Week, the growth of the aircraft industry in East and West Cowes, the return of the 'visitors', as my mother so charmingly called them, back to the seaside resorts of Sandown, Shanklin and Ventnor; Sunday School outings and, as everywhere else, the schoolwork and endless examinations.

For us Cowes Week began with the works siren at John Samuel White's blasting off its welcome as the Royal Yacht *Victoria and Albert* rounded Hurst Point with guardships fore and aft. Suddenly the town became alive with sailors in jerseys with the names of yachts across their chests: *Shamrock, Endeavour, Velsheda, Westward, Astra, Britannia* and *Evaine*. The air was filled with the smell of reefer jackets newly released from a winter spent with camphor balls, the scent of expensive cigars, the gold-embossed badges on the lapels of members of the Squadron. At Bekens the medicine chests for the yachts were filled and awaited collection; at Dear and Morgan, and at Shergolds, the coffee grinders and roasters worked overtime and so did we boys as we waited on Watch House Quay for the dinghies coming ashore for provision, to whom we would offer our services to 'Mind your boat, Skip?'

Cliff Michelmore

Then on Friday night the spectacular fireworks display would presage the end of The Week. As rockets soared and we chorussed 'Better than last year' we knew that in the morning the Cowes Roads would be emptied of the yachts and 'the gentry' would have gone away shooting on the moors or else be bound for Torquay and the next regatta. It was just as though the plug had been pulled out of the bath which had, a short while ago, been filled with lovely playthings.

What would remain? Uffa Fox would career around the High Street, Claude Graham-White could still be seen driving the Gar Wood speedboat *Gee-Whizz,* the grocers and wine merchants would take stock and complain that things were "not what they were" and we would be back to school.

Since my schooldays at Cowes the Island has changed. Beeching closed down the network of railway lines so that only the ex-London Underground trains run along the holiday coast and the enthusiasts remind us all of what things once were like when they have steam-ups at Havenstreet. We have traffic lights everywhere when once we had only the single set at Yarmouth; a piece of dual carriageway makes do for our own version of the M25, and it gets just as congested; we produce garlic, wine, a few aircraft, writers, painters, engineers, business men and women, and a distinguished pop musician of Level 42 who once worked on our family farm in Rew Street. But then the Island has always nurtured a variety of talented people, from the inventor of the hovercraft to the man who gave us Hooke's Law, from the father of the public school system to a dairyman's daughter who found fame in other ways.

Wherever I have travelled across the world I have constantly been reminded of my island home; this place has the 'same length of coastline as the Isle of Wight'; this one has a 'climate rather like that of'; the Ngorongoro crater is the 'same size as the Isle of Wight' and you would need

three of our Island to 'fill the Grand Canyon', and so on. I have never been able to forget 'home' wherever I have been; but then I have never wanted to. I have a library of books about the Island and this one will be a welcome and treasured addition to its shelves because it reflects a number of other people's views of our Island. I do hope that you will enjoy it as much as I have.

Steam trains at Havenstreet evoke the atmosphere of a bygone age

Preface

It was Robert Pomeroy who realized that this book needed to be written. As a key figure in the Surtees Society he knew something about publishing books of special interest and, as a member of the committee which brought out the Bembridge Sailing Club centenary edition of Du Boulay's *Bembridge Past and Present*, he learned that the Island was special in more ways than one. He enlisted the support of his sister, Rosamund, of Robin Colville and Roger Sawyer, and between them they clarified the aims of what was to be a charitable enterprise. At first a sequel to *Bembridge Past and Present* was planned, but that idea soon gave way to something which would embrace the whole Island.

It was decided that all the contributors to *The Island From Within* would either be those who live or work in the famous houses or institutions whose stories they would tell, or authorities on the aspect of Island life which they would describe. This policy proved to be successful and the collection is, therefore, a mixture of the subjective and the objective. Written by Islanders and Overners, it contains accurate historical detail on the one hand and reiterates some myths and legends on the other. All in all, it amounts to a composite portrait of the Island as Islanders see it and as it is seen by those who choose to come here whenever they can escape from their other lives.

All the authors and all those involved in preparing the final manuscript have given their services free; and some have gone to considerable expense to fulfil the obligations which they so willingly accepted. Any profit will be given to three charities: the Royal National Lifeboat Institution (I.W.), the St Peter's Trust for Kidney Research, and the Anti-Slavery Society for tke Protection of Human Rights (Isle of Wight Group).

Acknowledgements

With an entirely charitable enterprise it is difficult to sort out who exactly is thanking whom. As everything depended upon the sponsors, clearly they must come first; their personal generosity has been immense. Then all twenty-three authors must be thanked for their various labours of love.

Cliff Michelmore generously agreed to write a foreword; as a gilt-edged caulkhead with literary and other talents, he had unrivalled qualifications for this task. He gets a special word of thanks. So too does Ann Pilcher, who has moved in mysterious ways to make quite sure that this production saw the light of day.

Sarah Mason was photographer for *The Island From Within*. Adrian Searle, journalist and author, was responsible for collating the illustrations. The invaluable work of these professionals, who have donated so much of their time and effort to this publication, is greatly appreciated. (Other picture sources are individually acknowledged).

Others who must be mentioned are Dick Davis who gave his design skills, Ken Hicks, who has given valuable advice, Carly Dawkins, whose enthusiasm brought great encouragement when it was most needed, and Michael Cunliffe and Mary Cullimore, whose assistance with research has been invaluable.

Finally, the editor expresses his gratitude to Andy Newman, Public Relations Manager of Sealink UK IW Services, for all his help. But for his favours the burden of postage alone would have been crippling.

A sea of masts at Cowes　　(Patrick Eden/Island Life)

Sponsorship

Publication of The Island from Within was made possible by donations from:

Julian Allason
Colonel and Mrs J.A. Aylmer
Georgina and John Blight
British Telecommunications, PLC, South Downs District
Lady Fairfax of Cameron
David Gascoyne
Michal Hambourg
The Isle of Wight County Press; Managing Director, Robin Freeman
Mollie Lamb
Lloyd's Bank, PLC (Ryde branch)
Anne Mansfield
The Hon Mrs Sarah Mason
Midland Bank PLC (Ryde branch)
Sam C. Morris
Ann and Anthony Pilcher (Adgestone Vineyard)
Michael Poland, MFH
Major the Hon Robert Pomeroy
The Hon Rosamund Pomeroy
Erica Prean
John P. Rawlings
Don Robertson
Charles Sawyer
Rupert Sawyer
Sealink UK (IW Services)
Diana Tunnicliffe
and one who wishes to remain anonymous

The charities that will be the sole beneficiaries of the sale of this book have one common denominator: they all save lives. Messages of thanks have been received from each of them:

ROYAL NATIONAL LIFEBOAT INSTITUTION
ST PETER'S RESEARCH TRUST FOR THE CURE OF KIDNEY DISEASE
ANTI-SLAVERY SOCIETY FOR THE PROTECTION OF HUMAN RIGHTS

Beneficiaries

THE ROYAL NATIONAL LIFEBOAT INSTITUTION has had a long association with the Isle of Wight and with my family. Pulling and sailing lifeboats were launched mainly from the southern beaches of the Island from the 1860s until the 1920s, when they were succeeded by motor lifeboats operating from Yarmouth and Bembridge, added to in the last 25 years by inshore lifeboats on all sides of this island. My great-grandmother, Mrs Charles Seely, christened the first Brooke lifeboat and my father, General Jack Seely, the first Lord Mottistone, served in the Brooke crew for 40 years from 1893.

Throughout the last 130 years or so, the Island lifeboats with their gallant crews have achieved a splendid record of intrepid rescue under arduous weather conditions, and this continues today. On their behalf I thank all those who have contributed to this excellent anthology - *The Island From Within* - for the donation of a third part of the royalties on its sale to the R.N.L.I. I trust that it will be widely read.

THE LORD MOTTISTON
President, Isle of Wight Lifeboat Board

ST PETER'S RESEARCH TRUST provides financial support for research into all aspects of kidney disease, carried out in the St Peter's Group of Hospitals, Covent Garden, the specialist centre for uro-nephrological disease within University College, London. Work pioneered in these hospitals has led to major advances in this field; many techniques developed here are now in routine clinical practice throughout the world.

Much still remains to be done. Money is needed to support and expand our research programmes, which can help existing patients as well as those of the future. Transplants and dialysis are life-saving measures in cases of acute kidney failure. However, in some ways they may be said to represent the failure of medicine.

The ultimate aim is prevention and cure, before these drastic last resorts are necessary. The fulfilment of this aim lies in research. Thank you.

LADY MORRISON BELL
Vice-Chairman, St Peter's Research Trust for the Cure of Kidney Disease.

THE ANTI-SLAVERY SOCIETY, the oldest human rights organization in the world, has much unfinished business to do - an estimated 200 million people currently live in conditions of servitude.

It is therefore with great pleasure that I express the thanks of the Society, one of the three recipients of the royalties derived from the sale of this splendid anthology, to sponsors, authors and all involved in its production.

Their generosity is greatly appreciated; they can rest assured that the fruits of their labour will be well spent.

It is with confidence as well as gratitude that I commend *The Island From Within* to a wide readership.

THE RIGHT HON LORD WILBERFORCE CMG, OBE, Joint President, The Anti-Slavery Society for the Protection of Human Rights.

Old Quarr Abbey's ruins stand defiant before their 20th-century successor

Contributors

COLONEL J.A. AYLMER

(*Nunwell - The Softer Touch*) was educated at Wellington College. He served with the Irish Guards 1943-80 and saw active service in N.W. Europe, Palestine, Egypt and Aden. He was Military Assistant to Lord Mountbatten 1963-64. Commanded 1st Batallion Irish Guards 1966-68, Irish Guards 1968-71. He and his wife, Shaunagh, née Guinness, have one son and two daughters. The family moved to Nunwell House in 1982.

SIR REGINALD BENNETT, VRD

(*Overners - An Anthropological Survey*) was educated at Winchester and New College, Oxford. He joined the Island Sailing Club in 1929, when racing W.L. Wyllie's 14-footer, *Bonaventure*. Having been a pupil of Uffa Fox, he has raced *Shamrock V, Evaine* (12m.), Dragons, Darings, Redwings, Bembridge Club Boats, and many more. He won the first Round-the-Island Race (Island Sailing Club) and rounded the Island three times in Cowes Week, 1935: in *Shamrock V* twice and *Bluenose* once. He and his wife, Henrietta, née Crane, have one son and three daughters. The family lived in Bembridge 1953-77 in two houses and two houseboats – not all at once! He was Conservative Member of Parliament for Fareham 1950-79. Member of White's and Seaview Buffs; Commodore of the Imperial Poona Yacht Club.

DENIS BRADLEY

(*Quarr Abbey*) was educated at Downside and the University of Surrey, where he graduated in Mathematics. He entered Quarr Abbey in 1973.

ANTHONY CANTWELL

(*The Victorian Fortifications of the Isle of Wight*) was educated at Dulwich College and Wadham College, Oxford. He is Head of History at Ryde School and a lecturer for the National Trust, the Historical Association and the Workers' Educational Association. He is married to Rosemary Poole and they have one son.

With **PETER SPRACK** he has written several books and articles on the coastal fortifications of the Isle of Wight. Peter Sprack is married to Morfydd Lloyd and they have one son and one daughter. The co-authors have advised public bodies such as the National Trust and the Isle of Wight County Council on the preservation and restoration of Victorian fortifications.

LIEUTENANT-COMMANDER HARRY CHILLINGWORTH, RN

(*Yacht Clubs and Yachting on the Isle of Wight*) has lived in Bembridge since 1962. After retiring from the Navy he taught for 18 years at Bembridge School. For 40 years he has been sailing yachts and dinghies on the Solent. As well as being a member of Bembridge Sailing Club, the Royal Naval Sailing Association and the Island Sailing Club, he is vice-chairman of the Isle of Wight Committee of the National Trust and a member of the Council of the Solent Protection Society.

JAMES COLVILLE

(*Centurion's Copse*) was educated at Harrow School. His family (which includes two other *The Island From Within* authors - see below - Robin, his brother, and Lady Pigot, his sister) have Island links which go back eight centuries. His wife is Virginia, née Horn, and they have a son and a

daughter. He has had a life-long obsession with the subject of his contribution, and has written on similar matters for local magazines.

ROBIN COLVILLE

(Two poems: *Bembridge Sailing Club* and *Royal Corinthian Y.C.*) was educated at Harrow School. After some years with Lloyds Bank and the Stock Exchange (member 1970-73) he is now director of a building franchise operation. His deep Island roots, mainly in Cowes and Bembridge, are reflected in his fifth generation membership of the Royal Yacht Squadron. His other clubs are Brooks's, Pratt's, Bembridge Sailing, Imperial Poona Y.C. and the Bombay Bicycle Club (Cleveland Ohio branch); he is a Freeman of the City of London and a Liveryman of the Fishmongers' Company. He was part-author of three reviews performed at Bembridge Sailing Club.

LIEUTENANT-COMMANDER BILL CURLING, VRD, RNVR

(*The Island in the Second World War*) was educated at Eton, after which he pursued a career in journalism until he joined the RNVR just before the outbreak of war. He served in the battleship *Rodney* and in several destroyers before he volunteered for Combined Operations and joined Force J as Assistant Signal Officer. He was based at Gurnard and then at Cowes until D-Day, when he landed at Port-en-Bessin. After the war he became Racing Correspondent of *The Daily Telegraph* ('Hotspur') and retained his links with Fleet Street until 1966. He has had eight books published, nearly all about horses, especially those belonging to members of the Royal Family. He is married to Elizabeth, née Bonham, and they have three sons and one daughter. The family has had a house on the Island since 1926.

JAMES S. DEARDEN

(*J. Howard Whitehouse and the Ruskin Galleries at Bembridge School*) comes from Cumbria and for many years collected books relating to the area (including those of John Ruskin). He was educated at Bembridge School, where he found many opportunities to absorb Ruskin's influence. After a break of eight years, in 1957 he returned to the school, where he now teaches printing and is Curator of the Ruskin Galleries. He is also Curator of the allied collection at Brantwood, Coniston. His published works include innumerable books and articles about Ruskin. He is a Companion of the Guild of St George, and Secretary of the Ruskin Association. He is married to Jillian, née Cheverton, and they have one daughter.

ALAN DOE

(*The Railways of the Isle of Wight*) was educated at Brockenhurst School and Bristol University, and is now Head of Geography at Bembridge School. A life-long love of railways led to his becoming a volunteer signalman of the Isle of Wight Steam Railway at Havenstreet. He is married to Carol, née Peters, and they have a son and a daughter.

OLIVER FRAZER

(*In Pursuit of Natural History*), who was educated at Dulwich College, took part in the D-Day and Arnhem landings as a member of the Glider Pilot Regiment. After the war he taught Biology and General Science on the Island and became lecturer, broadcaster and author. His offices and achievements have included: President of the Isle of Wight Natural History and Archaeological Society (1960-63); author and presenter of the BBC's 1974 series *What's in a Habitat*; co-author with his cousin, J.F.D. Frazer, of *Amphibians*; and author of numerous articles. His wife is Dorothy, née Newman.

PAMELA FREEMAN

(Some Painters of the Isle of Wight), née Bocquet, was educated at Hatchlands School, Upper Chine School and Reading University Fine Art Department. She started her career scene-painting for various ballet companies, including Ballet Rambert; she continued as a book illustrator and lecturer, and became well-known mainly for her detailed paintings of tropical flowers - she is still commissioned by Kew in this capacity. In a completely different capacity she was wooed by Frank Freeman in Kew Gardens, where he had taken her "to look for the Ginkgo tree"; he read to her from Burton's *Anatomy of Melancholy* in the Plant House. They had two sons and a daughter. Frank died in 1988.

DR JACK JONES

(Carisbrooke Castle) read History and Anthropology at Jesus College, Oxford, before going into museum work. He was Curator of Carisbrooke Castle Museum from 1953 until his retirement in 1984. His doctoral thesis was on *'The Isle of Wight, 1558-1642'*, and his books include *The Royal Prisoner: Charles I at Carisbrooke*; *The Isle of Wight: An Illustrated History* (jointly with his wife Johanna, née Lloyd); and *Isle of Wight Curiosities*.

KAY McDONALD

(Queen Victoria and Osborne) is married to Surgeon Captain Ronald McDonald, OBE, the last Governor of Osborne. She has always been interested in history; as a mature student she spent six years at Southampton College of Art studying Embroidery (its design and history) and was awarded the College's Advanced Diploma. With her husband she lived at Osborne from 1974 until 1985, and whilst there her interest in Victorian design and embroidery was developed. She now spends much of her time studying, teaching and lecturing part-time. The McDonalds have a son and a daughter.

LIEUTENANT-COLONEL PHILIP MITCHESON

(The Isle of Wight Foot Beagles) was educated at Aldenham School. He served in the Indian Army until the transfer of power in 1947, having been awarded the DSO for his part in the Italian campaign and the OBE for his services in the Punjab at the time of the hand-over. He came to the Island in 1947 to help run his twin brother's prep school, Little Appley. In 1959 he was invited to whip in to the Island's Foot Beagles' pack, and soon became Hon. Secretary. At the age of 80 he became Master. His wife is (Eileen) Clodagh, née Johnston, and they have two sons.

HUGH NOYES

(Literary Connections with the Isle of Wight) was educated in England, Canada and the United States. Nevertheless, in spirit if not always in body, he has been an Islander since the age of one; his permanent address has been Lisle Combe since 1929. He joined the Westminster Press in 1952, shortly after the publication of his *The Isle of Wight Bedside Anthology*, and moved to the editorial staff of *The Times* in 1958. From 1967 until 1982 he was *The Times*'s Parliamentary Correspondent. In 1990 he became High Sheriff of the Isle of Wight. His wife is Judy, née Wilson, and they have one son and four daughters.

DENYS PEEL

(The High Sheriff of the Isle of Wight) was born in Ireland and educated in England, Switzerland and France. In 1934 he joined the family cotton firm in Egypt, where he acquired a flying licence. A year later, after a sailing holiday at Bembridge, he bought an aeroplane and flew it back to Egypt. He spent the war as a pilot with the RAF and his subsequent career was in civil aviation. In 1974 he retired to live on the Island at Tyne Hall. He became High Sheriff in 1981. In 1941 he married Cynthia Kendall. They have three sons.

LADY PIGOT

(Royalty and the Isle of Wight), née Sarah Colville, was educated at St Mary's School, Wantage. She is the widow of Major-General Sir Robert Pigot, Bart., CB, OBE, O.St.J, DL, a former High Sheriff and a Deputy Lieutenant of the Isle of Wight, and has a son and a daughter. Her own involvement in the Island includes being Chairman of the Isle of Wight Lifeboat Board, a member of the Board of Visitors of Camp Hill Prison and a member of the Local Review Committee for Camp Hill Prison. She is a Lady Associate Member of the Royal Yacht Squadron and a member of the Bembridge Sailing Club. (Her connections with royalty stem from her descent from families who have served the monarchy for over 300 years).

MICHAEL POLAND, MFH

(The Isle of Wight Hunt) has been a Master of Foxhounds since 1972. He was Master and Huntsman of the Isle of Wight from 1983 until 1988; since then he has been Joint Master. He and his wife Carolyn, née Longmore, have two sons and five daughters between them. They have been associated with the Island, largely because of sailing connections, since 1946. The family has had a house in Seagrove Bay since 1974.

MAJOR THE HON ROBERT POMEROY

(The Worsley Monument - Brading Sea-Mark - Bronze Age Remains) was educated at Eton and in Berlin and Dresden. After a short period in the City he joined the H.A.C. and his military career during the war was with the Welsh Guards (six weeks in Normandy, 1944; Major 1946). In 1947 the Army sent him to the Island to look after the Surrey Cadet Force camp at Yaverland Fort. At that time the Colegates lived at Hill Grove and he started crewing Club Boats for them. In 1953 he married Anne Colegate and they have two sons.

DR ROGER SAWYER

(The Fort and its Walk) is a retired prep school headmaster who now spends most of his time writing about contemporary slavery. As well as many articles he has written three books on the subject: *Casement: The Flawed Hero*, *Slavery in the Twentieth Century* and *Children Enslaved*. He had several reasons for agreeing to co-ordinate and contribute to *The Island From Within* and none was more important to him than the need to raise funds for the Anti-Slavery Society. In 1952 he married Diana Harte and they moved to the Island in 1960. They have two sons.

PATRICIA SIBLEY

(Newtown) has lived and worked on the Island all her adult life. She is the author of several novels and has written many short stories and articles which have been contributed to the BBC and to numerous periodicals. Her most famous work of fiction, *A Far Cry from Clammergoose*, was read on *Woman's Hour*. Among her non-fiction works are *Discovering the Isle of Wight* and *Isle of Wight Villages*.

Carisbrooke Castle

JACK JONES

There is an organic quality about Carisbrooke Castle: like Cotswold villages it seems to have sprouted naturally out of the ground on which it stands. Geologists might argue this point, objecting that the site is chalk and the building is Quarr limestone; but the rocks are near enough cousins to preserve a harmony of landscape. The castle on its small plateau above the valley of the Lukely stream looks and is right.

It has an engaging quality too, a reluctance to give up its secrets. Fairly detailed building and maintenance accounts take us back to the 13th century. Tantalizing scraps of chronicle references pierce the speculative mists of the early Norman period. Before that we depend on the trowel and the post-excavation boffinry of the archaeologist. The game of unknotting the past of this monument will go on for some years yet.

Domesday Book in 1086 seems to help, for it mentions under the King's manor of Alvington that a castle has appeared on a virgate of land there since Edward the Confessor's time. This seems to fit well with the picture of a Norman motte-and-bailey castle planted at Carisbrooke by William FitzOsbern to put the seal on King William's unwontedly generous grant to him of land in the Island.

FitzOsbern, though, was not first on the scene. There were intriguing traces of earlier masonry inside the Norman earthworks, and linking with this walling was a discarded inturned entrance on the east side, opposite to the present drum towers and gatehouse. The finding of a stray Roman coin near this early masonry led to the suggestion that this was part of the late 3rd-century chain of forts built for coastal defence by the Romans. The existing meagre evidence argued for this; logic argued against it, for the virtues of Carisbrooke do not include suitability for coastal defence. Moreover the Roman reaction to a fortification on a hill was generally to destroy it. They built their own forts from choice at sea level, as at Portchester.

A more coherent picture began to emerge as a result of the extensive excavations in and around the castle directed by Dr Christopher Young for the Department of the Environment, later English Heritage. Working, over the seasons, painstakingly down to the original surface of the chalk hill, the archaeologists found that the first traceable use of the site had been for Jutish inhumation burials dated by their interesting grave goods to the 6th century. It was in the Christian Saxon period, about the 10th century, that the fortification appeared: an earthen bank with its masonry revetment, enclosing the area of the present Norman courtyard but with its entrance on the east. Inside, under the present north lawn, were traces of a substantial timber hall. The whole array was a construction of the burh type, a civic bolthole from the Danes.

Looping across this area, and defending the north-east corner of it, was a much later feature: a large ditch and internal bank, post-1066, to which a second and outer ditch was later added. Here is our Norman work at last, and it would seem that William FitzOsbern had found the Saxon-fortified area the worse for wear, and settled for putting just a piece of it into commission. The interesting implication of this is that the large artificial hill of the motte with the stone keep on top seems to belong to a second phase: there is hardly space for both it and the inner ringwork bank to have been conceived simultaneously. The keep mound, then, seems more likely to date from the early 1100s, possibly as part of the reaction to the invasion by Robert of Normandy in 1101. Certainly the stone curtain wall round the courtyard followed soon after, being mentioned by a chronicler as having been recently completed in 1136.

The origins of the castle, then, still offer a sporting ratio of speculation to certainty, and it is cheering to find that so much of its story has still to be unfolded. As we come into the period of written evidence, however, there are frequent glimpses of moments of high drama. One such early ruckus came in 1082. William I had been away in Normandy sorting out his problems there, and leaving his half-brother, the ambitious Bishop Odo of Bayeux, to mind the English shop. Odo's particular design at the time was, allegedly, pursuing the succession to the current Pope Hildebrand (Gregory VII). A soothsayer had foretold that the successor of Hildebrand should bear the name of Odo, and Odo of Bayeux received the prophecy cordially and proceeded to foster his interests at Rome. Having done all he practically could through his agents there, he decided that the personal touch would be decisive, and from his base on the Isle of Wight he was preparing to set off with an assembly of Norman knights, including Hugh, Earl of Chester, who had been bribed or otherwise persuaded to back the venture. It was at this interesting stage that William returned to England, and made quick tracks to the Isle of Wight. There followed a tense scene in what the chronicler Ordericus Vitalis called the royal hall ('aula regalis') at Carisbrooke. Having recited Odo's misdeeds William ordered his knights to arrest the offender; but they hung back, pleading that they could not lay hands on a prelate of the church. The King then arrested Odo himself, with the comment that he was laying hands not on a bishop but on one of his earls. Game, set, and match to the King. In spite of protests from the Pope, Odo was kept prisoner at Rouen for the remainder of William's reign.

Then there was the siege of 1136, the only occasion on which the castle was captured in battle, though it was not taken by storm. It was now in the hands of the de Redvers family, and Baldwin de Redvers, the then Lord of the Island, having supported Queen Matilda in the civil wars, fell foul of King Stephen. Having been defeated by Stephen's forces at Exeter, Baldwin fled to his newly fortified castle on the Isle of Wight, well provisioned for a siege. It was not his lucky year. The anonymous author of the *Gesta Stephani* reports that the wells suddenly ran dry ('aquae subita superveniente ariditate exsiccarentur') and Baldwin had to escape across the Channel to take refuge with the Count of Anjou. The offending well shaft was presumably the one in the keep, without much penetration into underground water flow. Its 160-foot shaft travels first through 53 feet of the artificial earth mound before reaching the real ground level. The other well, sunk into the courtyard about this time, has an effective depth of 161 feet and apparently taps the stream that breaks surface as a spring near Froglands, to the south-west of the castle. This is the well with a large treadwheel, for long worked by a donkey for the slaking of the castle thirsts and for the diversion of such visitors as Celia Fiennes in the 1690s, and John Wesley and the composer Josef Haydn in the 1700s.

There were other notable occasions when the castle was sucked into the affairs of the nation: most famously or notoriously the ten months when Charles I was a prisoner there from 1647 to 1648, after his almost capricious choice of Carisbrooke as a haven on his escape from Hampton Court. For this brief period couriers, ambassadors, and secret agents beat a path to the castle gates or to its most private recesses; and the scene has not greatly changed since then. The walk round the ramparts is the same as that which was taken by the King for his daily exercise and the view from the wall – scanning over the Elizabethan defences, down to the village with its fine medieval church – is still much as Charles saw it. Although the King's private room, the Great Chamber, was substantially remodelled in the 1800s, it still has the Tudor fireplace – then fed with coal, rather than logs – round which, on that extraordinary Christmas Day in 1647, Charles and the delegates from the kingdom of Scotland hatched a secret treaty that was to be the basis of the second Civil War during the summer of 1648, the failure of which sealed the King's fate.

1648 was studded with abortive rescue and escape attempts, and a window, the scene of one of Charles's failed escapes, still overlooks the castle hill on the north. Poignantly, in 1650 - the year after their father's execution - his two children remaining in England, Elizabeth and Henry, were brought as prisoners to Carisbrooke. Drenched in the rain out on the bowling green, Elizabeth became ill and died on 8th September in a small room quite near Charles's second escape window in the north wall. Her stay in the castle was only three weeks, and she was buried in Newport parish church where her rediscovered tomb is now marked by a 19th-century monument and effigy. Her brother Henry stayed as a castle prisoner until he was released in 1653 to join his family in France.

To return to the qualities of the castle: because of its almost continuous occupation since Norman times, it is an unusually complete exemplar of the changing techniques of warfare. The 12th-century curtain wall, built for height rather than thickness, reflects the need at the time to keep out people rather than missiles. Scaling ladders were then the order of the day. The later medieval development of the deadly crossbow, particularly in use during the French

Carisbrooke Castle in a 19th-century engraving.   (Adrian Searle)

wars in the 14th century, has produced examples - some still surviving - of the crossed-slit loops for archers, giving an adequate if restricted view from inside, and virtually no view from outside. The first European use of cannon, again in the 1300s, produced its first reaction in the provision of modest gunloops, like upside-down keyholes, in the big drum towers at the front entrance. The rather inefficient hooped medieval cannons seemed at first to offer no threat to the defences themselves. By the 16th century though, the gunfounders' art had progressed to the point where the medieval walls were something of a white elephant, and in the 1590s, under threat of invasion from Spain, a mile-long system of sophisticated artillery defences was built as a new encasement to the castle. It cost a fortune; and it was never used.

Sometimes the progress of the castle's growth is recorded, with deliberation, in the masonry. The lofty Montacute tower, near the well-house in the middle of the courtyard, was built by William of Montacute, Earl of Salisbury, then Lord of the Island; and his connection is duly recorded by a carved coat of arms on the corner buttress: a row of three lozenges (originally red) on a shield (originally silver) representing sharp mountains,

the usual punning rebus on the subject's name, Montacute. During the Wars of the Roses in the 15th century the then Lord of the Island, Anthony Woodville, had his coat of arms, flanked by a Yorkist rose, carved on the crenellation at the top front of the gatehouse. During the great remodelling of the castle defences in the 1590s the builders scattered a few carved dates around the outer wall, and as the work neared completion they duly carved the new south-east and south-west knights, added to the corners of the south medieval wall, with the dates 1601 and 1602 respectively. Some of the carvings, though, seem unofficial. On the stone lintel of the great 14th-century fireplace in the main hall some graffito artist has carved some heraldic shields, and added the name Bray in a 15th-century hand (this was indeed the name of one of the Island Captains about that time). So vandalism gently becomes history.

Not only the buildings tell their story: stray finds fill in the tale; finds like the crossbow boltheads that are found from time to time buried in the ground outside the castle walls, some of them with a stub of the wooden arrow shaft still in the socket. The castle had its biggest siege in 1377, about the date of these items. A French

A prison for Charles I ...a priority destination for the modern-day tourist

army overran the Island, besieged Carisbrooke and in fact failed to take it; but there are souvenirs of the battle still in the ground. Then there was the gold coin of Philip II of Spain, found during excavations in the keep moat. Sir George Carey, the Island Captain at that time, ran a small privateering fleet out of Newport harbour, against Spanish ships. Clearly, on this evidence, his operations were not without reward. Another find hints at a dash for freedom in the 17th or 18th century. The old medieval gates that used to hang at the inner end of the main entrance had in them a small wicket door just wide enough to let one person through. Embedded in the woodwork half an inch above this wicket was a sinister, squashed, musket ball. Presumably a sentry took exception to someone leaving, fired, and missed. Those medieval gates are stored away now, and their removal tells yet another story. In 1965 H.M. The Queen came to the castle for the formal installation of Lord Louis Mountbatten as Governor of the Island. The navigational channel between the medieval gates was rather narrow, and the risk of the royal car sticking midway was unthinkable; so the gates were taken off, with much groaning of block and tackle.

Throughout its history the castle has been the home of first the medieval Lords of the Island, then the Captains in the 16th century, and from the 17th century the Governors. The last Governor to live at Carisbrooke was H.R.H. Princess Beatrice of Battenberg, the youngest daughter of Queen Victoria. After her death in 1944 the Governor's House became a museum. Those Governors who lived in the castle may have endured some discomfort: indeed the Earl of Southampton - Shakespeare's patron - who made the experiment of residence after his appointment in 1603, wrote sourly to a friend in September 1605: "The barrenness of this place affords nothing to discourse of but heat in summer and storms in winter - which is now with us begun". Others took a rather more expansive view; and indeed the castle has a friendly atmosphere, gentle and beguiling. H.L. Mencken once remarked that "castles, sunsets and women never reach their maximum of beauty until they are touched by decay". It is probably the flavour of quiet obsolescence that now makes Carisbrooke so appealing.

Royalty and the Isle of Wight
SARAH PIGOT

Visits to the Isle of Wight by members of today's Royal Family are invariably happy occasions, whether they are of an official or sporting nature. Unfortunately this has not always been the case.

An early example of this must have been the confrontation between William the Conqueror and his half-brother, Bishop Odo, at Carisbrooke Castle (as described by Jack Jones, above). In 1082 Odo organized an expedition to Rome to overthrow the Church and seize the Papacy. His fleet was stopped in the Channel, on William's orders, and Odo was arrested - not as bishop (for no man would dare to lay a hand on a priest) but in his title of Earl of Kent. Odo's foray ended with his being removed to safe custody in Normandy.

Some 120 years later King John came to the Island. He arrived in Yarmouth in 1206, stayed three days, and then sailed for La Rochelle with an invasion fleet which had been assembled in Portsmouth. He paid a further visit to Yarmouth in 1214 when he was on his way to Poitou where, together with the Count of Flanders, the Count of Boulogne and the Emperor of Germany, the intention was to crush France and divide it up between them. They did not succeed. He is also reputed to have fled to the Island in 1216, after the signing of Magna Carta, landing near Fishbourne at the site which is today known as King's Quay.

Edward I came to stay at Swainston in 1285 and spent a week there as the guest of Bishop John de Pontiserra. The Bishop had been appointed by the Pope and the King used this as an excuse to quarrel with him. To quote Albin's *History of the Isle of Wight*: "the King deprived John de Pontiserra of this manor because the Pope had forcibly intruded him into that See, contrary to the King's inclination and pleasure ...... At length, the Bishop, to purchase the King's peace, agreed not only to surrender the manor of Swainston into his hands, and for himself and his successors for ever to quit claim to the said manor, but to pay a fine of two thousand pounds...." Sadly, the Bishop had to comply with this extortionate demand.

In 1293 Isabella de Fortibus, who held the Lordship of the Island, surrendered it to Edward I in return for the payment of 6,000 marks. The Island thus became part of the English realm and was no longer a semi-independent fiefdom. Within a year of its incorporation Edward I declared war on France. All landowners with property valued at over £20 had to provide an armed horseman for the Island's defences. Edward further demanded the services of the Island's knights to fight for him against Scotland. This they bravely refused to do, saying they were not bound to the King's service beyond the Solent.

Edward II tried to make his favourite, Piers Gaveston, absolute Lord of the Islanders by granting him the Castle and Honour of Carisbrooke. Not unnaturally he was not accepted by the Island's nobility.

There is an interesting Plantagenet/Tudor connection with the Island. William Hollis of East Standen, who was the son of William Hollis of Little Budbridge and Elizabeth Urry (d. 1492), had a daughter Joan (b. 1465) who married Thomas Cook. Joan and Thomas Cook leased Great East Standen to Princess Cecily, the daughter of Edward IV and Elizabeth Woodville. She had married in 1503, as her second husband, Richard Keynes, who is believed to have lived at Keynes Court, Niton. She died in 1507 and was buried at Quarr; but unfortunately her grave has now disappeared.

Joan Cook's grandmother, Elizabeth Urry, having been widowed, married George Bramshott and by him had a son, William, who married Emmeline Hacket. Emmeline's daughter, Elizabeth, was a godchild of Queen Elizabeth (wife of Edward IV). Emmeline's sister, Agnes, married Sir John Leigh of Appuldurcombe. Their daughter, Ann, married Sir James Worsley, who was a page to King Henry VIII, and became Governor of the Island. They and their descendants occupied Appuldurcombe for the next 300 years. Their son, Richard, also Captain of the Island, married Ursula St Barbe who, upon Richard's death, married Sir Francis Walsingham, Secretary of State to Queen Elizabeth I.

Henry VII was another Royal visitor to the Island, coming here in 1499 to stay with Dame Bowerman at Brook House (not the present house of this name but an earlier one on the same site). He also stayed with the Oglander family at Nunwell whilst overseeing the strengthening of the Island's defences.

Henry VIII came to the Island, accompanied by Lord Cromwell, to stay with Richard Worsley at Appuldurcombe. The King went hawking but unfortunately had poor sport which was put down to poaching. On his return to London the furious King issued the following Royal Edict: "It has come to Our notice that Our games of partridge and pheasant within Our Isle of Wight are much decayed by the sufferance of such lewd persons as, contrary to Our laws and pleasures, do daily take the same with nets and other engines." He went on to impress upon Sir Richard that partridges and pheasants must be "cherished within Our said Isle for Our disport and pastime" and that he and all other landowners must "spare the said game in your grounds and specially abstain from suffering any pheasants to be taken with nets and such engines as totally destroyeth the breed." The King's words were superfluous as he never returned to the Island but happily there are plenty of pheasants still.

James I and his son, Prince Charles, aged nine, landed at Cowes on 2nd August 1609. They saw a muster of forces at Honey Hill, then went to Carisbrooke, and on to Parkhurst Forest where they killed a "bocke". It is probable that some of the forces they saw were in fact young boys as Sir John Oglander wrote in his diary: "we met him at the waterside, where we kissed his hand" and that "he was much taken with seeing the little boys skirmish whom he loved to see better and more willingly than men."

This must have been one of the happier visits to the Island of the young Prince (later Charles I). He paid a further visit in 1618 and amused himself at Carisbrooke by "making divers shots with the ordnance."

War with France broke out in 1627 and Charles came over to Nunwell to visit troops billetted there, preparatory to an attack on the Ile de Rhe. The Governor of the time, Lord Conway, did not visit the Island to receive the King but left the task to the Deputy Governor, Sir John Oglander. The latter spent the day with the King and later noted down a list of things promised for the Island's defences - new forts, more arms and ammunition for the Home Guard and a squadron of ships to be permanently stationed off the Island. At the end of his list Sir John wrote: "so much promised and how happy we, if performed."

By 1642 the Civil War had started and before long the Island was under the control of the Parliamentarians. The Earl of Pembroke had been appointed Governor with Colonel Carne as his Deputy but in August 1647 Colonel Robert Hammond was made Governor. Colonel Hammond was a convinced Parliamentarian, the son-in-law of John Hampden, and owed his appointment to Oliver Cromwell. Both the Royalist, Sir John Oglander, and the Roundhead, Colonel Hammond, were stunned by the King's arrival in the Island on 14th November 1647 after his escape from house arrest at Hampton Court. He spent his first night in Cowes and the following day moved on to Carisbrooke, being presented with a rose whilst passing through Newport by little Frances Trattle, the daughter of a washerwoman. This event is commemorated by the Rose and Crown, a public house in St Thomas's Square, Newport. On 18th November he went to stay at Nunwell for his last visit as a comparatively free man - the menu included sweetbreads, whiting, oysters, prawns, cod, shrimps and woodcock - the bill for which, together with the wine, came to £1.15s.

Moving to Carisbrooke the King found himself a close prisoner. The next five weeks were taken up with much political parleying between the King and Parliament. The King, having rejected Parliament's terms and whilst Colonel Hammond was seeing off the Commissioners, decided it was time to escape. He put on riding boots on the pretext of going hunting in the forest but with the intention of making a quick get-away by boat. Unfortunately for him, this escape plan was thwarted for two reasons. Firstly, a quick look at the weather vane showed the wind was in the wrong direction for France and, secondly, Colonel Hammond returned.

The King had two more attempts at escaping. The first failed because he got stuck between the bars whilst trying to get out of the window (he had in fact been given a file with which to cut the bar but had discarded this on account of the noise it might make). The second attempt failed because, having managed to escape from his room, he found that the bank below was swarming with troops - two of the Roundhead guards who had been bribed to help in the escape had in fact reneged and told an officer of the plan.

Under the Treaty of Newport in 1648 Charles was released on parole and on 6th September he took up lodgings in Newport. Negotiations went

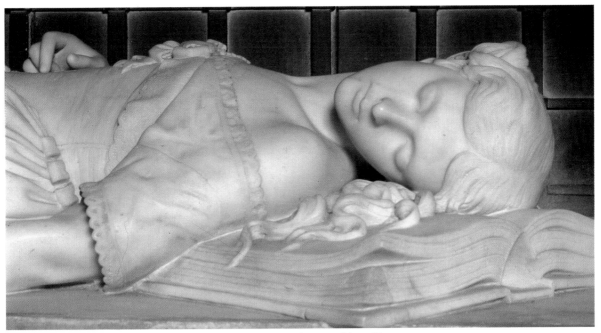

Princess Elizabeth ... Marochetti's striking monument in white marble at Newport.

on for two months and towards the end of November matters were resolved by an Army coup. On 30th November the King was arrested and taken off to Hurst Castle via Yarmouth. A little over two months later he was beheaded.

The King's association with Carisbrooke was not over though because on 16th August 1650 his daughter, Princess Elizabeth, together with her brother, Prince Henry, was sent to live there. On 19th August she was caught in a sudden shower whilst playing bowls on the green that had been made for her father. She became feverish and died on 8th September, holding the Bible that had belonged to the King.

The Princess is buried in St. Thomas's Church, Newport. A monument was erected by Queen Victoria which shows the Princess sleeping with an open Bible beneath her head which, according to tradition, was an invariable practice of hers. The inscription reads: "To the memory of Princess Elizabeth, daughter of Charles I, who died at Carisbrooke Castle on Sunday September 8th 1650 and is interred beneath the chancel of this church. This monument is erected as a token of respect for her virtues and of sympathy for her misfortunes by Victoria R. 1856."

Prince Henry lived on in captivity until 1653 when he was released and allowed to join his family abroad.

Some years were to pass before King Charles II came to the Island. He is on record as having made several visits. In 1665 he "landed in the Isle of Wight at Saint Helens pynt and rode to Carisbrooke Castle and dined ther and staid ther four hours." In 1671, 1675 and 1677 he visited Yarmouth and stayed with Sir Robert Holmes, the Governor of the Island. On what must have been his last visit on 8th September 1684 he came from Southampton to Yarmouth, killed a stag at Thorley, and was entertained by Sir Robert Holmes in his house at Yarmouth (now the George Hotel) where he "honoured William Stephens of Bowcham in ye withdrawing room." The story goes that he spent the night at Shalcombe Manor.

The Island seems to have been rather neglected by the later Stuarts and the Hanoverians until Princess Sophia and the Duke of Gloucester (children of George III) visited Cowes in 1811 and stayed for three months. The recently defunct Gloster Hotel (formerly the Gloucester Hotel and acquired by the Royal Yacht Squadron as its club house in 1825) probably owes its name to this visit.

The formation of the Yacht Club in 1815, re-named the Royal Yacht Club in 1820 and the Royal Yacht Squadron in 1833, with its subsequent royal patronage, put Cowes firmly on the royal map where it has remained ever since. The Prince Regent became a member in 1817, followed the next year by the Dukes of Clarence and Gloucester. In 1820, the Club asked the new King George IV to become its Patron. Since that day the reigning King has always been the Admiral of the Squadron but Queen Victoria was, and Queen Elizabeth is, the Patron. Following a successful visit to Cowes in 1819 the King returned in 1821 and rented a cottage on the seafront.

The long connection of Queen Victoria with the Island has been covered by another contributor. However, her descendants have also always played a leading part in Island life. Her youngest daughter, Princess Beatrice, was married to Prince Henry of Battenberg in 1885 at St. Mildred's, Whippingham, the church designed by Prince Albert. After a two-day honeymoon at Quarr Abbey, then a private house, they returned to live with the Queen at Osborne. Prince Henry was Governor of the Island from 1889 until his death, from malaria contracted during the Ashanti wars, in 1896. He was succeeded as Governor by Princess Beatrice who continued in this office until her death in 1944. After the Queen died the Princess lived in Osborne Cottage but from 1912 she used Carisbrooke Castle as her summer home until the outbreak of the Second World War.

Throughout his life King Edward VII, first as Prince of Wales and then as King, was a frequent visitor to Cowes as well as to Osborne. He was elected to the Royal Yacht Squadron in 1865 and became Commodore in 1882, a position which he held until 1900, becoming Admiral on his accession to the throne in 1901. He owned several yachts which he raced at Cowes, including the 205 ton *Hildegarde* and the famous *Britannia* which he had built in 1892.

Following the death of Queen Victoria the new King rather abandoned Osborne and in 1902 he gave the property to the nation. In 1903 Osborne became the Royal Naval College and amongst those who passed through it were the future Kings Edward VIII and George VI and Prince Louis of Battenberg, better known later as Lord Louis Mountbatten, the last Governor of the Island.

King George V was a frequent visitor, both to Osborne and to Cowes to race *Britannia*. Within a month of his marriage to Princess May (Mary) of Teck in 1893 he, with his bride, came to Osborne. On the evening of their arrival there was a dinner for fifty-five in the Durbar Room and the Princess sat next to the Emperor of Germany who himself often came to Cowes to race his yacht *Meteor* (the former *Thistle*, America's Cup challenger in 1887).

King George VI and Queen Elizabeth, with the Princesses, visited Cowes in the Royal Yacht in 1938, anchoring off Gurnard. They visited the Squadron one afternoon, which visit "was greatly appreciated. His Majesty was surprised at the multitude of small yachts and expressed his pleasure at the obvious popularity of yacht racing." A particularly historic visit was paid to Cowes by the King in 1944 when he took the salute from the Squadron battery as landing craft from Force J for the D-Day landings passed by.

Since the War and particularly in the last twenty years or so, the Island has had large numbers of royal visits. Hardly a Cowes Week goes by without Prince Philip being present for a few days, usually on board *Britannia*. Princess Alexandra and her husband are often on board as well and the Prince of Wales, Prince Andrew, Prince Edward and Princess Anne have all been here for Cowes Week. They have all sailed and raced enthusiastically, particularly Prince Philip in *Bluebottle*, the Dragon given to him and the Queen as a wedding present by the Island Sailing Club, in *Coweslip*, the Flying Fifteen which was a present from the people of Cowes, in *Bloodhound* and more latterly in a *Yeoman*, one of several which he has chartered from Sir Owen Aisher for Cowes Week.

Leaving the yachting scene aside, practically every member of the Royal Family has been to the Island in recent years. To mention but a few of such visits, the Queen installed Lord Mountbatten as Governor of the Island in 1965. She and Prince Philip visited Osborne, Westland Aircraft, the Royal Victoria Yacht Club, Ventnor, Shanklin and Sandown on one day, and Yarmouth on the second day of her visit. In 1987 they were both here again to mark the occasion of the Australian Bicentennial celebrations.

The Queen Mother was here in 1975 when she visited the Ventnor Botanic Gardens, attended a Service of Dedication for the windows in St Lawrence Parish Church and opened Glamis Court for mentally handicapped adults.

Prince Charles made a highly successful visit on a beautiful June day in 1982 when he opened the Needles Old Battery, unveiled a bust of Lord Mountbatten in Newport and opened the Mountbatten Centre at Medina High School.

Prince Andrew, as a boy, spent several summer holidays in Bembridge and later came over with the then Miss Sarah Ferguson to start the Schneider Trophy Air Race from Bembridge Airport.

Princess Anne, in her capacity as President of the Save the Children Fund, visited the Island in

1978 and again in 1988, and showed keen interest in the work of Riding for the Disabled on both occasions.

The Duke and Duchess of Kent have been over several times, mainly in connection with the R.N.L.I. The Duke has visited the lifeboat stations at Bembridge and Yarmouth, seen self-righting trials of a Rother Class lifeboat and in 1977 went to Yarmouth to name the Arun class lifeboat *The Joy and John Wade*. Five years later the Duchess visited Yarmouth and went out in the lifeboat.

Princess Alexandra named the Arun class lifeboat *Sir Max Aitken II* at a ceremony in Cowes in 1984, and the Duke and Duchess of Gloucester and Prince and Princess Michael of Kent have all carried out engagements in the Island.

The Princess of Wales was unable to accompany her husband in 1982 but in 1985 she opened Adelaide Court and Adelaide Club for the Elderly and visited Sandown Fire Station.

Quite apart from members of the English Royal Family who have been to the Island one must not forget that a large number of foreign royalty have also been here.

In August 1830 the exiled Charles X of France arrived in Cowes with his family and suite. On the 19th of that month the Duchesses of Berri and Angoulême could be seen walking on the beach while temporary lodgings were being sought for them in the town. They eventually decided upon the Fountain Hotel.

King Alphonso XIII used to come to Cowes in the Royal Yacht *Giralda* in order to race his 15-metre *Hispania*. In more recent years a visitor was his son, the Count of Barcelona, father of the present King of Spain.

Napoleon III of France came to Cowes and was elected a member of the Royal Yacht Squadron. After his fall from power in 1870 his wife, the Empress Eugenie, escaped from France in the yacht *Gazelle*. By command of Queen Victoria the Empress was received by Lord Colville who had a house in Cowes - it is a romantic coincidence that he had been very much in love with Eugenie when they met in Spain some 27 years before. Some months later Napoleon III was released from captivity and before retiring to die in Chislehurst he rented a house on the Green in Cowes.

As mentioned earlier, the Kaiser was a visitor to Osborne and also to Norris Castle, where he stayed when racing his yacht *Meteor* in the Solent. His Royal Yacht *Hohenzollern* was a

Princess Margaret visits the Island in the spring of 1990
(IW County Press)

frequent visitor to Cowes, acting as a tender to *Meteor*. She was part of the procession which escorted the body of Queen Victoria across the Solent from Cowes to Portsmouth.

Another who came to Cowes before World War I was the Tsar of Russia who presented a prize for 15-metre yachts.

Among more recent Royal visitors have been King Constantine of the Hellenes with Queen Anne-Marie and Crown Prince Harald of Norway. King Constantine is often here during Cowes Week as a guest on board H.M. Yacht *Britannia* and recently he was here in his capacity as Vice-President of Honour of the International Yacht Racing Union. Prince Harald was here as a member of the Class Policy and Organization Committee of the I.Y.R.U.

Of necessity this is a very brief sketch of royal connections over the past 900 years - some have had tragic endings but in the main they have been happy associations. This is particularly true of the last 150 years and one hopes that these bonds will be strengthened over the years to come.

The High Sheriff of the Isle of Wight
DENYS PEEL

In 1974 the Isle of Wight became for the first time a county in its own right, and in March of that year its first High Sheriff, Lieutenant-Colonel Richard Kindersley, D.S.O., M.C., D.L., of Hamstead Grange, received a letter from the Clerk to the Privy Council which read:-

AT THE COURT AT BUCKINGHAM PALACE
PRESENT
THE QUEEN'S MOST EXCELLENT MAJESTY IN COUNCIL

WHEREAS HER MAJESTY was this day pleased, (by and with the advice of her Privy Council), to nominate you for and appoint you to be HIGH SHERIFF of the COUNTY of the Isle of Wight, you are, therefore, required to take charge of the COUNTY and duly perform the duties of HIGH SHERIFF during HER MAJESTY'S PLEASURE, whereof you are duly to answer according to the Law.

Shortly afterwards, in the Crown Courts in Newport's Guildhall, he took the Oath, solemnly swearing to serve the Queen, reading out the ancient and enigmatic wording of the High Sheriff's Declaration.

Before 1974 the Island was a part of Hampshire and consequently came under the Lord Lieutenant and the High Sheriff of that county; although for centuries there had been an Island Governor appointed by the Sovereign. When the Island became a separate county the Governor, Earl Mountbatten of Burma, was appointed to the Lieutenancy, and Sir John Nicholson became the Vice Lieutenant; undertaking in fact most of the official duties of the Lieutenancy. Following the tragic death of Earl Mountbatten, Sir John took over as Lord Lieutenant, serving in that post until he retired in 1985.

A Lord Lieutenant serves until he retires, whereas a High Sheriff serves for only one year - a fact for which he may well have reason to be thankful as it can be an expensive year. Both posts are honorary, unpaid, and the persons involved are appointed by the reigning monarch.

In earlier days the High Sheriff, whose ancient post dates back to Saxon times, was the monarch's representative for law and order in the county, and the Lord Lieutenant was the military representative. The latter position originated in the mid-16th-century when Henry VIII wanted another person of authority whose duty was to raise the militia in each county.

The High Sheriff, although he was a commoner, took precedence over the Lord Lieutenant, who was usually a noble; and this situation remained until 1906 when, very reasonably, it was reversed by King Edward VII.

Today the High Sheriff's official duties are few and mostly ceremonial. No longer does he have to attend executions, appoint juries or read the Riot Act; but he does have to attend on the judges when the court is in session, preferably sitting with them for a few days. He is still the returning officer for the county at a general election, and he also has to attend on royalty when they make an official visit to the county where in precedence he follows the Lord Lieutenant. He is assisted by an Under Sheriff, who is normally a solicitor and who handles all the legal work such as serving High Court writs and issuing possession orders to the bailiffs.

On the more important occasions, such as an official royal visit or the opening day of the courts at the beginning of the legal year, the High Sheriff will be correctly dressed, that is to say in the uniform or the ceremonial dress of a deputy lieutenant or of one of the armed services, if so entitled; or alternatively in court or morning dress.

Apart from these few official duties he may during his year devote himself to any projects of public interest, especially on the subject of law and order. He normally visits the prisons and the police headquarters to familiarize himself with the law and order establishments. He is also expected to entertain the judges and to give at least one garden party or reception. He would also be well advised to join the Shrievalty Association from which he can get valuable advice.

The origins of the office of Sheriff date back to Saxon times when the peasant farmers elected a 'Shire Reeve' whose job was to administer the agreements made between them and the local lord. The 'High Reeve' or 'King's Reeve' was the person appointed by the monarch to run his estates and castles and to arrange for his entertainment and protection when he visited the shire. After the conquest the Norman kings adopted the Saxon system, but gradually appointed Normans to the post.

Over the years the Sheriff became a very powerful man, the peak probably being in Plantagenet days. He not only ran the monarch's estates but also was responsible for collecting taxes, running the courts and prisons, raising the militia, organizing elections and organizing and attending executions – of which there were plenty, the death penalty being the appropriate sentence for what today would be considered trivial offences. Many executions were looked on as a form of public entertainment. He not only was powerful but could become very rich. When the Norman kings started selling the post to the highest bidder, the Sheriff had to raise enough money not only to recoup his stake, but also to satisfy the king's treasury and to make enough to keep himself in a manner and style appropriate to his position. His chief sources of revenue were the peasantry and the church, and some Sheriffs could overstep the mark and their victims may have had good reason to look on them with less than affection. The peasants were mostly illiterate, so what they said of him is not recorded, but the monks could write and they have left one record of their views on a particular Sheriff of Cambridge (Picot) which appears in the *Libris Eliensis* in Ely Cathedral, describing him as a "prowling wolf, a crafty fox, a dog without shame who stuffs his belly ...", an opinion which may have a touch of the bias of a taxpayer against a tax collector.

In the reign of King John one Sheriff found a novel way to raise money from the church, a method found amusing by the monarch. He would kidnap the mistresses of the clergy and return them only after a ransom had been paid.

Despite a few black sheep among their ranks, High Sheriffs had an extremely demanding job, and if they had not administered it with energy and competence to the satisfaction of the King and the Treasury, they would not have held on to it.

Perhaps the lowest point for the High Sheriffs was during the days of the Stuarts in the seventeenth century. So profligate and rapacious were the Stuart monarchs and so great were the financial demands that they made on their High Sheriffs that in many cases every effort was made and every string pulled to get out of being selected - seldom with success. The King also found it convenient to rid himself of a tiresome opponent in Parliament by making him a High Sheriff whereby he could no longer sit as a member. One person who managed to escape being made Sheriff was Sir John Oglander of Nunwell who in 1622 was the Lieutenant Governor of Portsmouth. The Governor who appointed him was the Earl of Pembroke who was also the Lord Chamberlain. In reply to a request from Sir John that he should not be made Sheriff that year Lord Pembroke granted his wish. However, his luck was not to last. In 1637 the Governor of the Isle of Wight, Lord Portland, wrote to say that the king was insisting that he take up the appointment of High Sheriff of Hampshire, although agreeing that he could continue to reside at Nunwell. This was bad news for Sir John as it became his duty to collect King Charles's unpopular "Ship Money" tax from property owners. As a consequence he lost most of his friends.

The qualifications, apart from the need to reside in and own property in the county ("sufficient to answer the Queen and her people") are mostly negative ones. He may not be over 70 years old, or a practising lawyer or solicitor, a serving officer in the Forces, a Member of Parliament or a peer, an officer of the Post Office, Customs or the Inland Revenue, a priest, a convicted criminal or the guilty party in a divorce. This excludes quite a number.

There is no reason to prevent women from being nominated. There are records of two famous female High Sheriffs from history. One was the doughty Dame Nicola de la Haye, High Sheriff of Lincoln in 1216, who defended Lincoln Castle against its invaders. Another was Lady Ann Clifford, High Sheriff of Westmoreland in 1605. Both these were, however, hereditary holders of the post. More recently there have been female High Sheriffs in a number of counties - including the Isle of Wight.

The county roll is submitted to the senior presiding judge of the circuit, thence to a meeting of the Lords of the Council of the Queen's Bench Division of the High Court in London; finally to the Queen in Privy Council who selects her choice of High Sheriffs by "pricking" their names on the roll with a silver bodkin. Normally the name on the top of the list can expect to be appointed.

The origin of the "pricking" of High Sheriffs is supposed to have been on an occasion when Queen Elizabeth I was sitting in the garden with her attendants doing her needlework with a silver bodkin when the Lord Chamberlain approached and requested her as a matter of urgency to come inside to make her choice of High Sheriffs. The Queen remained seated and asked to see the roll, whereupon she pricked with her bodkin a hole in the roll against each name she selected. This method must have continued, and there is a picture in the Mansell Collection dated 1845 showing Queen Victoria with her Privy Council pricking the Sheriffs' roll with a bodkin.

The Isle of Wight is England's smallest county and, in common with a number of others, does not have a High Court wherein the major criminal cases are tried, and where the judges wear red robes. Ours is a Crown Court presided over by a circuit judge who is robed in black. The judge's long wig is seldom worn now, even in High Courts, but it is worn on ceremonial occasions. For example, it is worn on the Isle of Wight for the ceremonial procession to the Courts on the opening day of the legal year.

In 1974 the first three High Sheriffs were nominated and put on the roll by the Lord Lieutenant. Following Colonel Kindersley the next two were Rear Admiral Blackham, who had earlier been chairman of the County Council; then Mr John Britten, the designer of the Britten-Norman 'Islander' aircraft. Subsequent names on the roll were added one at a time by each High Sheriff after he had taken office. Following John Britten came Air Commodore Michael Birkin, General Sir Robert Pigot, Mr E.G. Feben and Mr Michael Clarke. In 1981 the writer was sworn in as the Island's eighth High Sheriff and to give some indication of the activities involved I can but relate my own experiences.

The Declaration which I read out when taking the Oath in front of the few people gathered in the Guildhall courtroom at ten in the morning in early April, was probably as cryptic to them as it was at least in part to me. It was clear that I promised "well and truly to serve the Queen's Majesty and preserve the Queen's rights; to do right to poor as well as rich; to do no wrong to any man for reward, favour or hatred. To serve the Queen's writs and take no bailiffs into my service that I cannot answer for. To diligently

execute the good laws of the realm, and well and truly behave myself in office for the honour of the Queen and the good of her subjects". It was less than clear what was meant when I declared that: "I will not assent to decrease or conceal the rights of the Queen or her franchises; that I will not respite or delay to levy the Queen's debts for any reward or favour where I may raise the same without great grievance to the debtor. I will take nothing whereby the Queen may lose or her rights may be disturbed injured or delayed; I will truly set and return reasonable due issues of them that be within my bailiwick, and make due panels of persons able and sufficient and not suspect or procured as is appointed by the statutes of this realm".

Whatever the meaning, it should not worry incoming High Sheriffs because all legal responsibilities are undertaken by the Under Sheriff, Mr Kilroy, who is a solicitor in practice in Winchester, and who is also the Under Sheriff for the county of Hampshire.

I was concerned that the Island did not have its own County Under Sheriff and started some investigations to see whether this could be changed. He has to fulfil all the duties in connection with the serving of writs, and with the sending in of bailiffs to take possession. His office also helps with the social calendar and the functions of the High Sheriff. As practising solicitors the Under Sheriffs are paid for the services they give, the costs being met from the poundage on the writs. The information I got indicated that in this law-abiding Island there are so few writs served that the poundage would not cover the costs and any shortfall would have to be made up out of the pocket of the High Sheriff. But a more important fact is that the law does not allow the Island to have its own Under Sheriff.

An Order (SI 222.1974), made under the Local Government Act of 1972, ruled that, although the boundaries of each sheriffwick will conform to the new county boundaries, those of the Under Sheriffs' bailiwicks would remain as before. Where an overlap occurs, the duty of the High Sheriff to appoint an Under Sheriff will fall on the one who has the larger county (after consultation with the High Sheriff of the smaller county). So, without further action by Parliament, the Island remains within the Bailiwick of the Under Sheriff of Hampshire.

After the swearing-in ceremony, which subsequent High Sheriffs have made more of an

The Island's present High Sheriff is Hugh Noyes.
(IW County Press)

'event' - and in some counties it is made a full dress affair - the most important landmarks of his year in office are the ceremony of the opening of the Crown Court, any royal visit to the county, and the High Sheriff's big reception.

The principal day in the High Sheriff's year is the one in early October when the crown courts are officially opened at the beginning of the legal year. The judge takes part in a procession with the High Sheriff, Under Sheriff and officials of the court, proceeding from St. Thomas's Square to the Guildhall; a distance of a few hundred yards. Up to 1981 they would forgather before the procession at the Wheatsheaf Inn where they would have coffee and the judge would dress up in his robes before stepping out into the Square.

I thought that this was a rather undignified start to proceedings when I recalled having been present at a similar event in a county with a High Court which had started with a short but spirited service at the Cathedral. The judge's arrival and departure were heralded by a fanfare played by the High Sheriff's trumpeters with their trumpets bearing banners embroidered with his coat of arms. That service opened with the stirring words: "Let justice roll down like water and righteousness like an ever-flowing stream", and followed with the splendid old bidding prayers.

After seeking the agreement of the presiding circuit judge that he approved of and would attend a similar service at St Thomas's Church, Newport, I appointed the vicar of St Thomas's, Canon Buckett, as the High Sheriff's chaplain, and together we worked out a short service using the bidding prayers, a couple of rousing hymns and finishing with a trumpet fanfare played from the chancel, followed by the National Anthem.

The fanfare was performed by four trumpeters of the Royal Artillery Band from Woolwich. They were in full dress uniform, and from the chancel steps played a fast, close-harmony fanfare. Then, after the anthem, they went round to the Guildhall where, from the balcony over the main entrance, they sounded another fanfare as the judge's procession arrived. Most of the well known military bands will provide such a service - for a standard fee. However, there is plenty of local talent on the Island (but not, of course, full ceremonial uniform).

After the anthem the procession formed up in the Square; the correct order is for the judge to be in the rear preceded by the High Sheriff and his chaplain, then the Under Sheriff and officials of the court, with a police officer leading.' The police stop the traffic and spectators line the route to the Guildhall. Once in the courtroom the officials take their places and all stand for the entry of the judge and High Sheriff who bow to each other and take their seats. The Sheriff is normally in uniform or court dress, and wears his sword as a token of his duty to defend the judge and to keep order in court.

The court dress that I wore was borrowed from one of my family and the colour of its silk velvet was midnight blue, not black - which was surprising considering that it was made in 1886 (I did not think that midnight blue came into fashion until the 1930s). The date I discovered by finding in the knee-breeches a label of the tailor in Buxton who had made it in that year for the High Sheriff of Derbyshire. The ceremonial sword had its Toledo blade engraved with the name of the High Sheriff of Anglesea 1922; I was glad that

I was not really expected to use it.

The Court rises at one o'clock and the Sheriff's next duty is to take the judge and senior court officials to lunch. I had arranged lunch at the Royal Yacht Squadron.

During 1981 there was one royal visit. His Royal Highness Prince Michael of Kent came to open the South Wight Leisure Centre at Sandown, and Princess Michael came to name the 12 metre, *Victory 83*, our Americas Cup challenger, which was moored bow-on to the quay at Souter's Yard at Cowes. The Princess, who has taken such a bashing from the press in recent years, performed her job with grace, charm and efficiency and a delightful touch of unscheduled enterprise when she kicked off her shoes and leapt on to the deck of *Victory 83* to chat to some of the crew who were on board.

1981 was the Year of the Disabled, so in addition to visiting the police and prison establishments, I made arrangements with the Director of Social Services to visit the homes for the handicapped, the family centres and homes for the elderly. I also visited the hospitals in company with our Member of Parliament.

A High Sheriff's most expensive day is the one on which he gives his reception; otherwise he has only to give a few lunches or dinners mainly to entertain the circuit judges. In general they prefer to be entertained informally in one's own home rather than in a place of public entertainment. Although there are a few rules of etiquette that should normally be observed about their arrival, introductions, entry into the dining room and where they sit and who should be served first, our Island circuit judges are not stuffy, and do not mind if protocol is not followed exactly. By contrast, one High Court judge, seeing the food served first to his wife, seated on the right of the High Sheriff, ordered its immediate removal and for the service to start again, bringing the dish first to himself.

For the big reception, if the High Sheriff's house is suitable, it is appropriate to hold it there. In my own case, Tyne Hall, Bembridge was a suitable setting with ample car parking space. It was an evening in October and a large marquee was erected on the lawn, one side of which was joined to the house by a covered way, the other side opened on to the floodlit lilypond and fountain. Invitations had been sent to over 300 people, of whom about 200 were officials, and the rest just friends. The guests were an-

nounced by the Island's Chief Toastmaster in his scarlet uniform and about 250 came. Between them they consumed twelve cases of Moet Chandon, half a case of whisky, some soda water and two glasses of ginger beer. The food was provided by the Hayloft restaurant of St Helens with their unique flair for providing the unusual (alas, they have now given up). After the party a gale partially blew down the marquee during the night, so we had been lucky.

The Isle of Wight is a new county and consequently does not have a long tradition of past High Sheriffs. It is also a low key county having no High Court so there is less pomp and ceremony than in some of the larger counties. There are 33 counties with High Courts. Nevertheless, apart from his few official duties, there are many things in which the High Sheriff can reasonably interest himself and possibly be of assistance, be it in the area of law and order, social services, Red Cross, St John Ambulance, schools, hospitals, British Legion or charitable organizations. His interest in an organization, and any visits he makes, are always appreciated.

During his year he must, of course, be non-political, and if a JP, he may not sit on the Bench. Apart from these restrictions he may get involved in any project of his own choosing and will probably find also that he learns quite a lot from his year in office. In my own case, I was totally ignorant of the workings of the prison system, and a visit to the three Island prisons, two of them top security, was most interesting, as was a visit to the Police Headquarters to learn about their organization which, because we are an island, has certain differences from the mainland.

In recent years there has been talk about abolishing the office of High Sheriff and transferring his few remaining duties to others. 'Others' would most likely be paid officials, and the cost of such a transfer would fall on the taxpayer, whereas the High Sheriff meets his own expenses. Abolition would also put an end to what is probably the oldest secular office in the realm, the origins of which date back to the tenth century. This would be a pity, not only historically, but also because it would put an end to one more bit of the ceremonial pageantry which the British seem to like and usually do so well.

Unlike the hangman the High Sheriff still has a rôle to play, even if a limited one, and it might be of benefit if he were given a few additional duties.

Nunwell - The Softer Touch
TONY AYLMER

The South Front and Georgian East Wing at Nunwell.

Since my family came to Nunwell, it has been described by varying journalists as an "architectural cocktail" and as "one of Britain's loveliest homes". Both descriptions are true. The house has been added to pretty regularly by succeeding generations of Oglanders so it represents every style of architecture from the 16th to the 20th century; yet it all seems to jumble together happily and every room radiates a slightly different welcome. Its gift as a home is its adaptability. No room is vast and, whether one is reading by oneself or enjoying a large party, each is equally agreeable. No great master of architecture or design is associated with the house, which perhaps gives it its homely quality, but its real genius is in its siting - as *Nunwell Symphony,* written some 400 years after Oliver Oglander made his choice for a new house in

1522, describes it: "surrounded by venerable oaks, the delicate beauty of its wooded slopes, its distant peep of the Solent and the Sussex Downs beyond could scarcely be surpassed in any country in the world".

But enough of Baedeker descriptions - they are plentiful, of both the house and its garden. Most of these give credit for its creation to male Oglanders. In 1990 male dominance is declining, so let us consider what the chatelaines of Nunwell have contributed over the centuries.

In any Nunwell investigation the name itself is often queried and, though mentioned in the Domesday Book, its derivation is uncertain. By the site of the original house there is a strong spring and this, coupled with the lady's name, Nunna, is presumed to be Nunwell's origin. Certainly, contrary to Island mythology, no religious foundation has been associated with it. Oglander can be linked with Orglandes in Normandy. The Seigneur d'Orglandes, owner of the Chateau de la Hogue there, sent his son Richard in the train of William FitzOsborne, who took part in the Norman subjugation of the Isle of Wight, and his reward was a grant of land at Nunwell.

Today in Nunwell research one tends to go back to that most famous son of the Isle of Wight, Sir John Oglander (1585-1655). Doughty diarist and unswerving Royalist but also Lt. Governor of Portsmouth, High Sheriff, and M.P. for Yarmouth, he must have left many of the problems of running an estate to his beloved Frances More of Losely, whom he married in 1607. On their honeymoon they returned to Nunwell and reopened the house, which had been shut for over two years since John's father's second marriage. They improved it by modernizing it, and they created the garden. Had it not been for money problems life for them at this time would have been 'pure content': John was knighted by James I in 1615 and Frances bore him nine children. But even then Nunwell cost money to run and Sir John records "this year I have spent ready money £747.3s.5d. I *must* spend less". But a year or two later he was able to relax a bit: "It was a bad time on us both. But with God's blessing we rubbed it out and lived most contentedly. I could never have done it without a careful thriving wife, who was no spender and never wore a silk gown except when she went in company and never to please herself. She was up every day before me and oversaw all the outhouses: she would not trust her maid with directions but would wet her shoes to see it for herself".

The Island social scene at the time is depicted as serene. Twice a week the landowners would meet at a clubhouse on St George's Down to play bowls and dine. Sir John paints a robust picture of his friends in what he called "the paradise of England" - "a merry gang of gentlemen that loved a cup of sack and a pretty girl".

Unfortunately, however, sadness succeeded happiness in 1632 when his eldest son died of smallpox on a visit to Caen. The difficulties increased in 1637 when, as High Sheriff, he had to raise the King's ship money. His loyalty to his sovereign never failed. But his popularity with those who bore the taxes did. He was certainly not a popular figure when the Civil War broke out in 1642. At that time, most of the Island gentry were what in modern politcal parlance would be called "wet" and quickly trimmed their sails to the Parliamentary wind. Not so Sir John, a true friend of the King. That "merry gang of gentlemen" now looked the other way when they passed him and before long he suffered periods of imprisonment in London and heavy fines were levied on the Nunwell estate. Frances had no easy time coping with it all. She wrote to him in prison "our servants' meat will last but one week longer. The smallpox is come nearer" and, when some of the estate staff seemed to be not above a spot of blackmail, "your new shepherd said, if I would not let him have the keeping of 6 ewes for himself, he would not come". Sir John from his confinement tried to keep her morale up - "all that I desire of you is to bear it with good courage and not by your grief to let our enemies see you grieve".

But Frances was not a passive woman. She went to London and lobbied everyone her distinguished family knew till Sir John was released. The effort was too much for her and she died on 12th June 1643. As Sir John put it, "my poor wife overheating her blood in procuring my liberty died making me a worse prisoner than before - greater grief could not befall any man". It was, then, as a widower that Sir John had to receive King Charles I for his most famous stay at Nunwell on 18th November 1647. Wisely he recorded none of the conversation, but he did note that the provisions for the Royal visit cost £1.15s.0d. He died eight years later a rather lonely sage, but he had kept Nunwell in the family, and without Frances's support he might have lost it.

Recovery from the Civil War was slow and the next two generations only just managed to keep Nunwell going, despite the honour of a visit from King Charles II to the house on 31st July 1665 and a baronetcy "free from any payment" in regard for the family's great sacrifices for their King. Sir William (1st Bt.) and Sir John (2nd Bt.) and their wives had little scope to blossom. Dorothy Cheke, Sir William's wife, had a long widowhood marred by endless warfare over money with her daughter-in-law, the town-bred Mary Webb, who kept a very tight hold on the Nunwell purse strings. Although blessed with many daughters Mary only produced one son - William - in 1680. Sadly his father died when he was three and Mary died four years later. So in

Detail from a painting at Nunwell of Louisa, Lady Oglander, wife of Henry, the 7th Baronet. It was she who directed the excavation of the nearby Roman Villa.

1688 Nunwell's future looked parlous, an infant orphan having inherited an estate short of funds. But, as so often happens, from challenging roots great prosperity was to grow.

The distaff side of the family came to the rescue. Sir Robert Dillington of Knighton died in 1688 and his widow, Aunt Anne to the infant baronet, moved into Nunwell to care for the orphan and the house she loved. Will, as the third baronet was known, was blessed with ability and charm. At the age of nineteen he married Elizabeth Strode, his senior by seven years. The Strodes were a great Dorset family from Parnham and Elizabeth's father had been as fierce a Royalist as Will's great-grandfather.

Although approving of the Strode family, Oglanders were worried by the age imbalance and by the knowledge that Elizabeth was the thirteenth child of her parents; as she had nine elder brothers not much inheritance seemed likely. But Will and Elizabeth both loved Nunwell and family fortunes, thanks to sheep farming, were improving.

When Elizabeth's father died her mother, who was always known as Lady Poulett, was invited to visit Nunwell. The old lady was so enraptured with the house that she never left it till her death in 1710. She then provided a legacy, which enabled Elizabeth not only to transform the south front of the house by giving it a Queen Anne appearance, but to place over the stonework the Dutch mathematical tiles which so intrigue visitors today, and to add the first small east wing. But Elizabeth died in 1722; like all her family she died young. Will never remarried; he planted the great avenue of lime trees in front of the house as her memorial, and it stands today despite the great storm of 16th October 1987.

Will's son John (4th Bt.) succeeded in 1734. On a visit to his mother's old home, Parnham, in 1729 he had met and married Margaret Hippisley-Coxe from the neighbouring house of Ston Easton Park. She was renowned as a bad speller but intelligence was her great gift to her sons - one became a Fellow of All Souls; another, Warden of New College; and a third, a Fellow of Winchester. She died in 1746 leaving her husband to spend twenty-one years as a widower. But though these were lonely years for him 1764 saw the greatest improvement in Oglander fortunes. That year George Strode, his mother's last surviving brother, died childless and the whole Parnham Estate passed to John Oglander. He had no intention of leaving Nunwell but his eldest son Bill (who was to become the fifth baronet) had just married an attractive and rich wife, Sukey Serle of Testwood in Hampshire: Parnham was given to them as a wedding present. About this time Bill's sister married a respected barrister, John Glynn, and from this great consequence was to flow in the next century.

Bill and Sukey had just settled into the great house at Parnham when his father died. Their intention was to live at Parnham and to visit Nunwell occasionally. But after his father's death in 1767 a visit was essential and it was planned to stay for a month. The house exerted its usual charm on Sukey and all the plans were changed. Nunwell became their home and Parnham went into eclipse. Bill was at heart a classical scholar who ran his estate with efficiency and great kindness and did his county duties. But Sukey was Nunwell's greatest patron. The east wing as we know it today was her inspiration - built with the aid of an unknown local architect and modelled to some extent on Testwood. The ceiling in the library was a consequence of her trip to Florence and it was her initiative to bring back Italian craftsmen to do this work and the fireplaces. The library bookcases modelled on Chippendale and the original Chippendale furniture were all to her credit.

Despite all this she found time to have eleven children. The Hampshire Chronicle showed in 1788 what excitement was caused even by the birth of younger sons - "Lady Oglander was safely delivered of a son at Nunwell, on which occasion the villagers partook of the joy. The inhabitants of Brading proclaimed the event by the ringing of the church bells and on Sir William's attendance at the church every countenance bespoke a heartfelt pleasure ... the bells were rung again until Sir William had arrived back at Nunwell".

Their later years were clouded by the French Revolution; Sukey died in 1805 and Bill, it was said, of a broken heart a year later.

The sixth baronet, another William, was a rather silent bachelor, who inherited Nunwell, Parnham, a house in Portman Square, 24,000 acres and a large balance in the bank. His life was well ordered - spring and autumn at Parnham, summer at Nunwell and winter in Portman Square. But in 1810 he stirred himself to marry the Duke of Grafton's eldest daughter, Lady Maria Fitzroy, and to her Nunwell owes a great debt. Not only had William inherited a fortune but oak, so much in demand for ship-building, made him another one during the Napoleonic Wars - so cash was 'burning a hole in his pocket' and he was determined to spend some. John Nash was a friend of his and had rebuilt the stables at Nunwell. He now submitted a plan to William for more or less replacing the house with a grand Palladian mansion. William was tempted. Maria was horrified and by her feminine tact persuaded her husband that Nunwell should be left alone and Nash's energy diverted to Parnham, which he duly reconstructed, and some say ruined. This was Maria's greatest gift to Nunwell, but she gave her husband 42 years of happy marriage, dying three years after him in 1855.

Their surviving son, Henry (seventh Bt.), known as Pen, succeeded - a shy, introverted man, who loved Nunwell but whose overriding interest was sailing. When he was 35 he married Louisa Leeds. Sadly the marriage provided no children but Louisa's foresight in old age in directing the excavation of the Roman Villa at Brading has stood the estate in good stead. Now, for the first time in eight centuries, there was no Oglander heir. The worried Pen had a solution for the Nunwell estate in a Glynn cousin living at Fairy Hill, who had conveniently been christened

John Henry Oglander Glynn and, on inheriting the estate, he simply dropped the Glynn by deed-poll. Sadly, Pen was never interested in the Parnham estates and left them to a Fitzroy cousin.

John Henry had met his bride at a Nunwell garden party, a very rare event under Pen, on 18th June 1872 - the 57th anniversary of the Battle of Waterloo. Florence Somerset, staying with a cousin in Ryde, wrote naively in her diary that evening "we went to a rose show at a lovely place near here called Nunwell with a most beautiful view over the park to the Solent and the Sussex Downs. Met a Mr. J. Glynn who was very interesting and told me the names of all the roses". Romance bloomed from the roses and Florence next returned to Nunwell as Mrs Oglander. She was to help her husband run Nunwell for almost four decades and supervise the opening of the Victorian dining room and the building of the billiard room, as well as a reorganization of the gardens, the lodges and the hanging of the great front gates cast in Como. Their happy life was dimmed by the First World War, when the Hampshire Regiment varied the view by camping and training in the park before going to Mesopotamia. Their daughter Joan went to France as a nurse and wrote on 11th November 1918 "Isn't it wonderful to think it's all over ... and that wars are over for ever, and I shall soon be coming home to darling Nunwell".

Joan inherited the estate in 1924 as its first female owner and presided over it during times of tempestuous change. Her tenure coincided with a vast improvement of communications to the Island and her social scene was more national than insular. Sir John's "merry gang of gentlemen" had by now given way on the lawns to the bright young things of the inter-war years. At house parties they adorned the new tennis court and swimming pool as well as the portico outside the library, which the second Lord Mottistone designed for Joan. In the 1930s the house was let to friends for summer parties and amongst visitors at these were both Prince George and Prince Edward, the future King Edward VIII, whose ukulele playing in the billiard room, now reorganized as a music room,

kept visitors up till the small hours of many a morning.

But, despite the optimism of Joan's Armistice Day letter, the lights were soon going out over Europe once more. She saw Nunwell through the serious invasion dangers of the 1940s when her husband commanded the East Wight Home Guard in the long tradition of squires of Nunwell. The headquarters were in the cellars, and ammunition dumps replaced the garden borders.

The social revolution after this war affected Nunwell as it did so many other great houses. Staffing of pre-war standards became impossible and maintenance costs rocketed. It was a sadder Nunwell Joan's son Denys inherited in 1961. But he threw his energy into restoring it and replanting the gardens until he was overtaken by an incapacitating illness. His wife Peggy (née Erskine) took on the running of the estate and completed the conversion of Nash's stables and coach house into a lovely second house. Eventually the Oglander estate had to take a sad decision to sell the main house, which was deteriorating, and my family had the good fortune to come and live here. Like others before me, I am away much of the week and the burden of looking after and improving Nunwell falls on my wife.

As did Peggy Oglander before her, Shaunagh Aylmer (née Guinness) now makes a vast contribution to the artistic decoration of the house and the refurbishment of the garden, creating a house that can be lived in in the economic and domestic circumstances of today. Resident staff and big house parties are among Nunwell's memories, but happily nowadays a much wider public can glimpse its charms and keep its spirit alive.

The old house has coped with history and I am sure it will continue to cast its warm spell on all who live in it in the future, but I hope they will spare a thought for the long line of ladies who, in addition to motherhood, have given it so much. They have all contributed brains, wealth and hard work, but above all love and perhaps just a bit of magic to make Nunwell what it is.

Sir John would salute them all!

Queen Victoria and Osborne
KAY McDONALD

For over fifty years Queen Victoria and her family spent part of every year at her maritime residence, Osborne House, in the Isle of Wight.

The first eighteen of those years were blissfully happy, but after the premature death of her husband in 1862 came a time of mourning and desolation. This, however, was followed later by mellow happiness with the enjoyment of her Battenberg grandchildren. In all those years she came to the Island for her summer holiday and always for Christmas (except in 1886, when Princess Beatrice needed to stay at Windsor after the birth of her daughter). The Queen's descendants remembered those golden days by the sea and in the lovely gardens; and they are described graphically in books of royal memoirs.

That the Queen chose the Island for her private home was a happy chance. She had visited the Island in her youth, staying at Norris Castle. She sampled the spa waters at Sandrock, and toured the whole island with her redoubtable mother, the Duchess of Kent, for already it had an enviable reputation as a resort.

When the Queen came to the throne in 1837 her royal residences were far from satisfactory. Windsor Castle was an unhealthy and public place, Buckingham Palace in a state of disrepair, and her one house by the sea, the Royal Pavilion at Brighton, not at all to her taste and again vulnerable to public curiosity. Two years after her accession she had married her first cousin Prince Albert of Saxe Coburg and they immediately started a family. Neither had experienced a truly happy childhood, and they had plans to remedy this with their own children. A private home by the sea was talked of and in 1844 an opportunity arose to acquire one.

Lady Isabella Blachford, a widow whose only son had just died, was offering for sale Osborne House on the Isle of Wight, and, as this estate ran alongside the Norris estate, it is entirely possible that the Queen may have visited or at least seen the house. Sir Robert Peel recommended it for her interest at a purchase price of £30,000.

The Queen's recent travel by steam yacht (much preferred by a somewhat reluctant sailor!) removed any apprehension about future journeys across the Solent; and the advent of the railway system ensured that the Court could be reached easily by the Privy Council and Ministers. The prospect of a private home by the sea must have seemed very attractive.

When this possibility was being discussed in 1844 the royal couple had been married for four years and, with the imminent arrival of Prince Alfred, would have four children. To them Osborne House must have appeared to be an ideal residence. The attractive Georgian house was set in a pleasant park of some 200 acres with lawns gently rolling down to the beach on the Solent. Bordered by Norris Castle on one side and Barton Manor on the other, it offered both privacy and security.

So the matter of purchase was seriously considered. Lady Isabella's original price of £30,000 was not acceptable, and the Prince's agent offered to lease the property for £1,000 per annum with an option to purchase later for £28,000. This sum was to include furniture and fittings, but not works of art or paintings. This offer was accepted and on October 10th 1844 they moved in.

Predictably the house proved to be far too small - too few bedrooms and totally inadequate kitchens. An amusing picture is conjured up of the royal chefs trotting back and forth to the pastrycooks in East Cowes village to use their ovens when a reception or large dinner party was planned. However, the family were more than delighted with their new home. They loved the views of the sparkling Solent from their windows, the delightful walks in the gardens, the games on the beach; all these made it a holiday home of enchantment.

The Queen and the Prince realized, of course, that, if they did decide to buy, a great deal of money would be needed for improvements and extensions, although no public money was to be asked for. With the Prince's prudent revision of their expenses it was now possible for all to be paid for from the Queen's Privy Purse. It appeared that Prince Albert was, surprisingly, prepared to bargain, and now offered only £26,000 for the house. After a nerve-racking wait

Queen Victoria's water-colour of the Royal Children at Osborne in 1850   *(English Heritage)*

for a reply, this was finally accepted; a most fortunate outcome as the recent visit to their other marine residence in Brighton that year had been both uncomfortable and depressing.

Now visions of rebuilding rather than extending had been advised by Thomas Cubitt, who had been asked to advise on the house at Christmas 1844. The splendid prospects of improving and running a model estate were exciting for the Prince. His next move was to purchase Barton Manor. Much-needed extra accommodation would come with the house and extra acres with woodland and farms would offer more scope for the new landlord. One problem remained: Barton was already leased from Winchester College for the next seventeen years and an Act of Parliament was needed to release this; but then the purchase was made for £18,000, plus an annual rental to the college and the Bishop of Winchester, of about £130.

The new house must now be built and a period of great joy started for the young parents. The Prince could now put into practice his brilliant ideas on building and architecture. The Queen's pride in his achievements was great and she delighted in the general admiration of him. His great strength was in choosing the most suitable experts to help him. This had already been shewn in his choice of the master builder, Thomas Cubitt, instead of an architect. This was not a popular move with the Royal Institute of British Architects but the fact that it was a private commission made it acceptable. Moreover, the Prince had knowledge and very decided ideas, and the determination to put them into practice. Cubitt's organization was comprehensive and he could supply every need except for the interior decoration and gilding. This, together with the purchase of paintings and objets d'art, was to be the province of Herr Ludwig Grüner, the Prince's art advisor.

Queen Victoria and her husband had travelled extensively throughout the country since their marriage and had been entertained in the great houses of England. They soon became aware that the royal residences fell far short of the standards of comfort and convenience they had experienced on their travels. In the new house every attention was to be paid to comfort and the Prince intended to achieve high modern standards in heating and sanitation with the help of his brilliant builder. Sadly, the first major decision that had to be made was for the demolition of the old house, although it would be needed as extra accommodation until Barton Manor was ready for use, and the new family wing was completed.

Cubitt's greatest achievement so far had been the building of Belgravia and his style was recognizable and known to his royal patrons. Using many of his proven methods they decided on an Italianate style with two campaniles, the whole building cleverly planned to sit naturally into the site with terraced gardens facing the valley walk to the sea. For the house they produced a basic plan that was simple but for a royal residence quite unique. The Pavilion (or Family) Wing would be virtually a private family home, with attendants, visitors and staff to be housed nearby, but in separate wings, joined by corridors to the main building. The top floor of this building would be entirely for the royal nurseries, and the floor below would house the private apartments. The plan provided just one bedroom, two dressing rooms with modern bathrooms and lavatories, and, in addition, a sitting room for joint use. On this floor also were to be a schoolroom (closely under the parental eye) and a room for the governess. Apart from provision for the dresser and valet, this was all. The ground floor was to consist of three small interconnecting state rooms, a billiard room for the Prince, as well as the dining and drawing rooms. Suites would be provided for the older children and their attendants in the main wing.

As soon as Barton Manor was made habitable the foundation stone was laid for the Pavilion Wing. This was in June 1845 and by September 1846 the family, now with one more baby, Princess Helena, were able to move in. Cubitt's brilliant organization and attention to detail was rapidly producing that comfortable home. The house was heated by boilers in the basement, and insulation and fireproofing were together produced by packing layers of seashells and shingle between the floors. Craftsmen from all over the country were drawn to the Island, and brickworks and workshops of every kind established. A landing stage and jetty were erected on the beach, initially to enable barges to land supplies from Mr Cubitt's London ware-houses, but later for passengers from the royal yachts. The pier house was also the station for the coastguards who protected the shoreline for the Queen.

The household wing came next, extending to the east behind the old house. Here were rooms for Court officials and the ladies in attendance on the Queen. There was a splendid dining room and a billiard room for leisure hours, but the gentlemen of the household were housed at Barton Manor, and faced a tramp over the farm fields to duty and to meals. When this wing was completed the sad moment came for the demolition of the old house, but the stones of its porch were saved and re-erected at the entrance to the nursery garden as a sentimental reminder.

The main wing could now be built parallel to the household wing and it was extended at the farthest end to produce a ground floor set of rooms for the Queen's mother, the Duchess of Kent. Provision was made for guests as well as the elder children, but its finest feature was to be an impressive Privy Council room with an adjoining small Audience Room for the Queen. These two wings were to be joined to the Pavilion by a grand corridor with a covered arcade above it (destined to be the favourite playground of the royal children in inclement weather) and another corridor above, giving access from the nurseries to the top floor.

The terracing of the gardens was the next undertaking, but throughout all the upheaval during these major works the royal family came and went and the pattern of their life at Osborne was established.

Princess Helena and the four children who came after her were known in the family as the 'Osborne Set' for it was after their arrival that those joyous holidays began. There was great excitement when in 1853 an entire Swiss chalet was imported in sections and erected in the garden some distance from the house. In 1854 it was ceremoniously handed over to the children, fully equipped for play and learning. The girls were to learn to cook and sew, while the boys were to garden and learn carpentry under their father's tuition. Mr Cubitt's men had made miniature tools and wheelbarrows for all of them and marked them with their names.

Here again a unique situation existed. Whereas in fashionable families of that time the children were handed over almost entirely to nurses and governesses, the royal parents spent as much time as possible with their family. The Prince played with them, flew kites and devised delightful entertainments and the Queen found more and more excuses to drive down in the pony trap to sample the cakes and admire the gardens, and soon a desk for her was moved into the little sitting room. A swimming pool with a collapsible base was contrived in the bay and the young, who were looked after by sailors from the Royal Yacht, had tremendous fun. The Queen ordered a bathing machine to be made for her own use, and when it was winched down into the sea she could have her own sea bathe in complete privacy. Such joyous days they were - Victoria spending long days sketching and doing water-colours of the house and the children and continuing to work with Leitch, her drawing master. The children's tuition continued and the happy days on the beach were also planned to include collecting seaweeds and shells, and learning to mount specimens with Miss Hildyard, their favourite governess.

The Queen's attachment to the Island grew as she began to know it better. As well as making journeys of exploration and for picnics with the children, she started to visit the families on the estate and in the village, and also took an interest in the village schools. She was saddened by a visit to Parkhurst, which was then a 'House of Correction' for young offenders, for children as young as twelve years were punished by being put to the treadmill. She felt close to the people on the Island and in Balmoral (which had just become her Scottish home), but was never to become aware of the problems of the deprived masses in the cities.

Osborne was essentially a summer home, for as it was built to face almost due north some of the rooms were quite gloomy in the winter months. However, the Christmas holiday brought other delights and if there was snow it became a wonderland. Then Barton Manor was the centre of activity; there would be skating on the lake and tobogganing and surely snowmen and snowballs too! Christmas trees had been introduced into England by Queen Adelaide, and Prince Albert carried on the tradition, and the parties and the present tables were a wonderful sight.

This blissfully happy part of Queen Victoria's life came to an abrupt end with the sudden early death of her husband on December 14th 1861, and she was never to be that happy carefree person again. Because she retired to Osborne to mourn immediately after the tragedy a picture grew of the house as a permanent place of mourning. This was far from the truth, for the pattern of the royal family's life shortly resumed, and the regular visits to Osborne began again. Short visits to Cimiez in the south of France were also added to the royal round at this time, after

the Queen had gone their initially to inspect a memorial to her son Leopold. Of course she did remain desperately unhappy, but even during those first ten depressing years, her children and then her grandchildren sampled the delights of her holiday home by the sea.

Queen Victoria's sad but dutiful life continued through the long years of her reign and the Golden and Diamond Jubilees were celebrated. It was to Osborne that she came for Christmas 1899, feeling old and unwell, and it was there, in the room that she had shared with her beloved Albert, that she died on January 22nd 1901.

When her son was crowned as Edward VII he gave Osborne House to the nation as a coronation gift. He had inherited Balmoral from his mother and already had a country home at Sandringham. His visits to the Island would mostly be on the Royal Yacht as he was a keen sailor and he intended to keep Barton Manor for the use of guests. He made a proviso that the two large wings of the house become a convalescent home for officers of the Army and Royal Navy, and a naval college be established in the grounds, and that the Pavilion Wing be a permanent memorial to his mother, with access for the public to certain rooms.

In 1974 my husband, a medical officer in the Royal Navy, was appointed as House Governor of Osborne House and as Medical Superintendent of that Convalescent Home. We came to live in the Pavilion Wing in what had been the royal nurseries and for over eleven years had the privilege of being a part of that great house. It was to be the end of an era, for at the end of that period the house was to be divided. English Heritage were to look after the state apartments and the convalescent home was to be the responsibility of the Benevolent Fund of the Civil Service.

We were fortunate in arriving at the beginning of a long period of refurbishment and re-decoration and as we saw the Pavilion Wing returning to its former splendour we also began to learn more about the family who had lived there. For this was a truly Victorian house and unique as a royal residence in that only one sovereign had ever lived in it. No other taste prevailed. There was still the reputation of an unhappy house linked to that sad and elderly widow. The clue to the real feel of the house was a splendid portrait in the state dining room of the Queen, Prince Albert and their five children,

painted in 1847. This was the family who first lived in Osborne. These were the happy ghosts of the house, and the sad little figure in mourning came much later as that Empress of India for whom the last wing of the great house was built. This building provided a large banqueting hall and was as Indian in character as the rest of the house was Italian.

Five children are shown in the portrait: Victoria, Albert (Bertie), Alice, Alfred and Helena. There were four more to come: Louise in 1848, Arthur in 1850, Leopold in 1853 and Beatrice in 1857. Princess Alice in fact was married in this dining room in 1862. Her father had admired and approved of her prospective bridegroom, Prince Louis of Hesse, and so the Queen agreed to allow the wedding, but it would have to be a private affair so soon after Prince Albert's death. Sadly, she listened from her bedroom above to the preparations being made for the ceremony and confided to her diary that night her desolation - for Princess Alice had been very close to her father, who would have been so happy to see her marriage.

In the following year it was to Osborne that Princess Alexandra of Denmark (the prospective bride of Prince Edward) was bidden to be 'vetted'

by the Queen. She passed this test with flying colours and it was to Osborne that the newly-wed couple returned after their short honeymoon.

Swiss Cottage looked as it had been when the royal children were pursuing their hobbies and developing their skills. The studio which had been provided for them on the 'Princesses Corridor' was now used as a sisters' duty room, but it was here that Louise was to be found not only skilled in drawing but an excellent sculptor. Prince Leopold, who would have lived on the floor above, pursued his interest in art here. He was the most delicate of the family and because of this spent more than the others at Osborne.

Despite her own unhappiness Victoria took a keen interest in her childrens' marriages, as in the many grandchildren arriving. Letters of advice were showered on her daughters and in fact the greatly loved eldest daughter, who was the first to marry, received a letter daily and was soundly berated if she failed to reply. Princess Victoria had married Prince Frederick of Prussia; only Princess Louise had married a fellow countryman (the future Duke of Argyll), and there were many letters to write. With eight of her children married into the European royal houses she truly became the 'Grandmama of Europe'.

The strongest bonds with the Isle of Wight were formed with the marriage of her youngest child, Beatrice. When the Queen reluctantly allowed her close companion to marry Prince Henry of Battenberg, she did so with the condition that they lived with her; she was increasingly infirm and had come to rely completely on Beatrice. A departure was made from tradition and a village wedding was planned in Whippingham Church, which had been rebuilt by her beloved Albert. It was a very happy occasion, with a reception in the Council Room and in the marquees on the lawn. Even the very short honeymoon was at Quarr Abbey, Lady Cochrane's house near Ryde, and it was to Osborne that they returned to start their lives with the Queen.

The four Battenberg children brought great happiness to the Queen, but this was to be blighted by the early death of Prince Henry. He died of fever on an expedition to the Ashanti and his body was brought back to be buried in that same Whippingham Church. The Island mourned a very popular Governor and Captain-General, who had also been Governor of Carisbrooke Castle.

The Battenbergs had lived in an apartment over the Durbar Hall, which in 1974 was the quarters of the matron and nursing staff of the convalescent home. After the latter was separated from the Pavilion the apartment became the province of English Heritage, while Princess Beatrice's sitting room is now a splendid education room used by the hundreds of schoolchildren who visit Osborne - an outcome of which Prince Albert would surely have approved.

Also at this time the Council Room was used as a smoking room by the convalescent officers, a privilege much appreciated and closely guarded - hence the provision of a separate sitting room for lady officers in the Duchess of Kent's suite. The Audience Room had become the House Governor's office and from all these rooms the view of the terraces and the valley walk offered a prospect which seemed to be waiting for those happy royal children to reappear. The two Winterhalter portraits of the young Queen and Prince dominate the Council Room and it is their presence which is felt in this part of the house, where the patients still dine in the green and gold Household dining room. But in the Indian Wing, lavishly decorated by Bhai Ram Singh and designed by Rudyard Kipling's father, it is that small elderly figure in black, so proud of being the Empress of India, whose presence is so palpably felt. It is easy to imagine her sitting in the Horn Room with an equally elderly lady-in-waiting among countless paintings of her favourite dogs. She was given to eating large meals very quickly, was overweight and gouty, but quite missed the point when her doctor suggested a liquid diet of Benger's Food to reduce, for she found it quite delicious and took it after a five course meal. It is this queen who is most easily imagined in the grounds taking the daily drive - which she did until a few days before her death - though in latter years someone would always walk beside her carriage to converse, as she did tend to fall asleep easily. She insisted on fresh air and kept most of the windows open, to the consternation of the Household.

She died a great queen, but was remembered by those who knew her in the happy Osborne days as a devoted mother and believer in family life. Her personality, in youth and in old age, is woven into the very fabric of Osborne House.

Newtown

Patricia Sibley

The raised footpath crosses the marshland at Newtown Quay.

Some hundred thousand years ago, between ice ages, great beasts roamed over this land - huge horned bison and elephants with six-foot tusks, but Newtown Creek first enters history with the Danish raid of 1001 when a shore settlement is said to have been burned and pillaged. The Bishop of Winchester later came to own the large estate of Swainston which included the creek and by his orders a new town was built on its banks with a grid of streets laid out as precisely as any 20th-century development, Gold Street and High Street running east to west, Broad Street and Church Street crossing them at right angles: between them the land was divided into burgage plots or smallholdings. While the tenants had to pay rent, they were free of the usual manorial duties and tithes, hence the name Francheville, or Freetown, the original name of Newtown on the east bank of the creek, founded in 1218.

The French raid of 1377 seems to have begun the decline of Newtown, though it had a mayor and borough charter still in 1598 and was returning two members to Parliament. A scheme to reclaim part of the marsh then fell through, but about 1700 a vast area of salt flats was enclosed by a bank with two sluices to control water levels. Part of the new land was used as salterns, for Newtown, despite its name, had become a mere village dependent on agriculture, fishing and salt making. At about the same time, though, a new town hall was built, for Newtown continued to send two members to Parliament until the Reform Bill of 1832. Albin, writing in the 18th century, said, "It is plain that the four members of Newport and Yarmouth are returned by only two persons. The members for Newtown are chosen at present by four persons: in all six members by six electors only". The population by this time was about 70 and the 13th-century church of St Mary Magdalene had fallen into ruin. During the early 19th century the town hall was used as a school.

The salt industry flourished, though; there were six sites altogether, including that at Shalfleet Quay and another on the eastern peninsula. The three largest would share a load of coal brought in by ship. A saltern consisted of several rectangular ponds, divided from the sea by high banks and filled with sea water a few inches deep: as the sun evaporated the water, what was left became strong brine. At Newtown this was drained off along a ditch into a pit near the brick boiling house, from which it was pumped up to the boiler - the pump was a hollow tree trunk with a wooden piston. Boiling crystallized the salt which was then sent off from the jetty by boat. It was the opening of the vast Cheshire salt mines which destroyed the Island's industry: the Newtown salterns closed down early this century.

Later, one of the salterns was used to breed oysters from spat, but conditions were wrong and the infant shellfish died. Nearby an attempt was made to grow asparagus, but this too died out. But over on the eastern entrance to the creek a brick-field flourished, and all through the 19th century a certain amount of river trade was carried on. Captain Holbrook, for example, sailed the *Wellington* to and from Dorset, bringing back cargoes of Portland stone for Island builders.

At the end of the last century the village had a resident colony of coastguards, a pub, several dairies and Woolgar's grocer's shop. The pub, properly called the Newtown Arms, became known locally as Noah's Ark, presumably because of the coat of arms above the door, depicting a leopard in a slightly ark-like boat. J.H. Woolgar, who kept the shop, wrote a little book about Newtown in the 1880s in which he says nonchalantly of one dwelling, "The house served its time but passed into decay and collapsed. This is the fifth house that has collapsed within the last twenty or thirty years to my knowledge". He also burst into verse:

The Town Hall stands on an eminence overlooking the harbour,
And in the past within its walls you might hear a good palaver.

Today, Newtown is a little hamlet scattered between arms of the creek, pasture land, hazel copses and salt flats, on the way to nowhere; its only large population the gulls, waders and geese out on the marsh, now protected as a nature reserve: a green and peaceful corner of the Island with little traffic even in high summer, and fascinating to explore on foot.

From Shalfleet the lane crosses a narrow stone bridge over an arm of the creek called Causeway Lake - to the west where it widens out stood the old quays, long disappeared, though the shapes still show up in aerial photographs. A narrow channel winds away between the mud flats, curlew crying in the distance: in winter flocks of black and white lapwing fly in, while August purples the banks with sea lavender. Not a house in sight ... Walk on down the lane, though, and there is the town hall, a sturdy brick building complete with balcony for announcing election results, and open to the public in summer: the wide grassy space on which it stands was part of Broad Street.

Just beyond lies one of the few old stone houses in Newtown, once the village pub, with the coat of arms still above its door. Here the tarmac lane turns to the left into High Street, but look to the right also and there is the eastern end of High Street continuing as a wide grass path.

The nature reserve's reception centre was moved here into the middle of the village about ten years ago, and a visit to it enriches any visit to the marsh itself. There are check lists of birds, displays of waders and gulls, a chart showing how the marsh develops its wealth of vegetation, maps and photographs of the village, a fifteen-foot fire iron used in the brickworks and, most spectacular of all, the fossils. The skull of a bison measures more than four feet from horn tip to horn tip, the tusk of a straight-tusked elephant at least six. These date from a period between Ice Ages, some hundred thousand years ago.

Along High Street stand a few cottages, old and new, and the village pump with a large iron wheel. This was the principal street of the town, as the name implies, and it is still possible to see the lines of some of the old burgage plots on either side where gardens or hedges still divide the land into small parcels, though this was more evident before hundreds of elms were lost in the epidemic of Dutch elm disease. At Woolgar's cottage the lane swings right - it once continued straight on down to the quay.

A church was built here at the time of the founding of the new town, and dedicated to St Mary Magdalene, at whose feast an annual fair was held, but this fell into ruin; the present small building, rather chapel-like, with a bell turret at the west end, dates from 1835. One of its most interesting features is a horrific drawing of the old church at about 1800, a roofless ruin with only three walls standing and all overgrown with trees.

The lane turns another right angle, out of Church Street into Gold Street, though the eastern length is gold only with buttercups. A footpath leads down to the marsh where the grass banks of the old salt pans still enclose shallow water where tern dive for fish, though the salt house is now only a heap of bricks.

Round about 1700 the marsh to the east was reclaimed. This must have been an enormous undertaking, involving the building of a sea wall and sluices round 120 acres in a blunt triangle, all of which became pasture land. A map of 1768 shows it as land "Property of Sir Thomas Worsley, Bart." with salt pans at the tip. All this was changed by the great tide of 1954 which breached the wall and flooded the pasture, returning it to mud flats. Ever since the quarter mile of remaining sea wall has been a much-loved walk, but at the end of 1981 a tide as high as that of 1954 with a north-easterly gale behind it made a fresh breach, allowing the sea into the salt pans.

But on the reserve there is an interesting new development. A few years ago ten pairs of little tern used to nest out on the Brickfields peninsula; then the numbers dwindled away to nothing, probably because of thoughtless picnic parties landing from boats. So it was decided to create a new and safer habitat to encourage the tern to come back. In the summer of 1980, with the help of a grant from the World Wildlife Fund, the Scrape was created. The word scrape, since it can describe the depression made by a bird for its nest, suggests some minor pond; the Scrape is in fact a wide lake with a high bank all the way round and a deep ditch outside to keep out predators. Four islands have been prepared to provide different levels of vegetation; for example, one is gravel over polythene to encourage little tern and oyster-catchers which favour an almost bare shore.

While there is plenty of nesting space on the reserve, many nests are lost every year, swept away by spring tides; in the Scrape the water level can be controlled so it is hoped that mallard, shelduck, ringed plover and redshank will move in too. A new hide overlooks the lake.

Newtown is still invaded. Every winter huge flocks of Brent geese fly in and browse for months around the grassier reaches of the creeks, often flying right over the village, darkening the sky with their wings and filling the air with a hound-like yelping. Herons and kingfishers fish the inland channels, while copseland provides a different habitat altogether.

The oyster fishery eventually moved from the village into the centre of Town Copse, where clams and oysters undergo their final cleaning in large tanks. Never mind coals to Newcastle, clams are now being exported from Newtown to the United States. The National Trust has wrought a great change in the copses by reviving the traditional method of coppicing, that is harvesting hazel, ash and thorn by cutting poles near ground level and leaving the tree to sprout anew, in a ten-year cycle. The neighbouring copse, Walters, used to be treated in this way and is now one of the richest in the Island, botanically speaking, with 140 different species - coppicing lets in sunlight, of course, and encourages growth on the copse floor. The poles were used largely for the making of sheep hurdles; now they are a useful part of coastal defences: made into mattresses and covered with rubble and planks, they help protect the sea wall from further encroachment by the sea.

Three Spots on the Island
ROBERT POMEROY

The impressive Worsley Monument on Bembridge Down.

The Worsley Monument stands on the top of Bembridge or Culver Down, nearly 350 feet up, where there are fine views to the north and the south–west, from what is now National Trust property. It is a tall obelisk, in stone, on an 18-foot square base and it shows the arms, supporters, crests and motto of the Earls of

Yarborough, whose family name is Pelham, and whose second title is Baron Worsley. The motto reads "Vincit Amor Patriae", which might be said to mean "Love of Country Conquers".

The monument is dedicated to the 1st Earl of Yarborough, (1781-1846), who sat in Parliament from 1803 to 1823 for Great Grimsby and then

41

Co. Lincoln; and who was the first Commodore of the Royal Yacht Squadron at Cowes. He died on his yacht, *The Kestrel,* in Vigo at the age of 65, a much-loved and generous figure, as the long inscription, albeit a fraction fawning, proves.

The nearby moated red brick coast defence fort of 1862-1867 is also well worth a visit. It was built in the days of Lord Palmerston to resist possible French aggression by Napoleon III. This seems strange, given that we had fought and won the Crimean War, 1854-6, with the French against the ever-expanding Russians – history repeated itself in 1945 when Stalin took five more countries, but was not stopped. This fort is also under the care of the National Trust and is used as business offices. In the 1860s and 1870s the guns, with a range of 8,000 yards, were manned by three officers and 100 men of the Royal Artillery in case the French arrived.

Brading Sea-Mark, in many ways a similar construction, lies just over two miles west of Brading, 429 feet up, on Ashey Down. A stark white obelisk, it is labelled G R II and dated 1735. Its purpose was, and still is, to help vessels (whether English or French!) including those which constantly ply between Portsmouth and the ports of France. As Hilaire Belloc has said in his *Cruise of the Nona:* one is only out of sight of land, sitting at the tiller, for about an hour and a half, the distance from, say, Barfleur or Cherbourg being about 70 miles.

The approach to the Mark is up a field track starting from the road junction near Ashey, and there are, of course, fine views to north and south. Just the place for a picnic, provided the cattle are not too inquisitive.

Bronze Age Remains at Shalcombe, half-way between Newport and Freshwater, and one mile north of Brook, close to the Down, now National Trust property, consist of a cemetery, tumuli and barrows.

In the *Encyclopaedia Britannica* of 1911 it is argued that the Bronze Age, which succeeded the Stone Age, was arrived at because of imports from the Eastern World. This may well be; and the debate continues as usual ... the ages do mix.

Nonetheless, the place has great charm, whatever anyone might say. Brook Down, 496 feet above sea level, as indicated by its trigonometrical point, comes now virtually in its entirety under the National Trust; but the lanes near Chessell with its pottery and Shalcombe, with its 18th-century manor house, are really romantic and, it seems, deserted, even by hikers, for whom a path is marked by the Isle of Wight County Council.

Cemetery? Tumuli? Barrows? Nothing is new, practically ... look in any churchyard today, for all three.

Mrs Elizabeth McKenzie-Walker, of Shalcombe, has kindly indicated her interest in the archaeological remains on her land, and would clearly give her blessing to investigations which any might wish to pursue (provided that they ask for permission first).

The ages, once again? They go, as all know, thus: Stone, Bronze, Iron. We, of course, today, are well into the Steel age – and the Plastic.

Any who wish more learning might consult Lord Avebury (1900), Sir John Evans (1881) and Chartre's *Age du Bronze en France* – no doubt of greater interest to citizens of the Isle of Wight. And much later stuff, too.

It is, of course, a question of man's civilization in its succeeding stages; and European implements, be they swords, awls, knives, gouges, hammers, daggers or arrowheads, are identical in pattern and size. Yes, things and people did come across the Channel!

Bembridge Sailing Club

ROBIN COLVILLE

Behind that sacred wooden door
Lies another world,
Where members drink and reminisce
And scandal is unfurled.
The steward and his merry wife
Cope with all with ease
Whilst Redwings glide across the sea
And Club Boats chance the breeze.

When high tide's early in the morn
To Under Tyne they go
By launch from waterlogged pontoon
To cheat the flood tide flow.
The ever tireless boatman
Packs the helmsman in,
From Commodores to Dinghy Boys
And fearless kith and kin.

There's Captain John, intrepid salt
And lady with head band;
Alone, a yachtsman at the bar
Has ginger beer in hand.
Commanders here and Colonels there
Sink pink gins by the score
And then go off to see the start.
But soon return for more.

There can be times when boats collide
And furious rows erupt;
The fellow sailing on port tack
Is thought to be corrupt.
A protest meeting is thus called
To sort the matter out,
But when decisions are complete
The answer's still in doubt.

Regatta day comes once a year
Towards the autumn fall
And many yachts from nearby clubs
Compete with one and all.
Occasionally a motor boat
Flashes by at speed,
And a serious sailor's heard to say:
"Well, that's just all we need."

But do not think it's all like this
There is a sober side.
The Clubhouse has a library
Where people go and hide.
A picture of the Colonel
Hangs upon the wall,
A gentleman of great esteem,
An example to us all.

Wild garlic covers the floor of Centurion's Copse.

Centurion's Copse
JAMES COLVILLE

Close to Bembridge Airport and approached by a public footpath leading from the busy main road to Sandown lies an area of woodland, reeds and undergrowth steeped in local legend and blended together with unconnected historical facts.

Even if one attempts to disregard the influence of hearsay and rumour attributed to this wood, there is a certain mystique and aura that may seem intensified when the traveller passes through the glades on such a day that a light air sends an all-pervading scent of wild garlic to his nostrils. It is at this moment that the traveller will recall to mind the history and legends of Centurion's Copse.

Yar Island, consisting of Yaverland and Bembridge, was until comparatively recently a separate entity from the rest of the Isle of Wight. Indeed, an early print shows a bridge joining the two, with Henry VIII's Sandham Castle in the background. Although a certain artistic licence may have been taken with the print, there seems little doubt from the alluvial deposits that the Brading Haven was once the bed of a very large river, or perhaps lake. For the purpose of portraying a picture of the Haven, it would be fair to imagine that, until the final reclamation of land in 1880, the upper reaches of the area were mostly very shallow at high tide, except in the navigable channels, and that at low tide there were large expanses of treacherous mud flats. Various reclamations of land have gradually, since the first in 1338, left areas of marsh and in some places even highly valuable grazing land.

There seems to be an argument as to how the name of Centurions' Copse is derived. Some claim that the land was once occupied by the Romans, but perhaps the more likely explanation is that relating to the fact that a chapel dedicated to St Urian occupied a site on a hillock close to the path leading down into the wood. It is interesting to note that in Sir John Oglander's diaries of 1588 it was even then called Centurion's Copse, a name which was acknowledged to be a corruption of St Urian's Copse. The Chapel of Wolverton, dedicated to St Urian, a Breton prelate of the 8th century, was next to the ancient manor house of the family of Clamorgan, and was certainly in existence up to the time of Edward VI, as is shown by the following from the Chantry Certificate:-

"The ffree Chaple of Seynt Uryth in Bymbrydge ffounded by Thauncesters of John Gylberd gentylman to thentente to have A prest to srve there (As yt ys supposedde) for the ease of them And theyr famylie ones in A weeke And for the Stipend of the said Prest He gave yerely xls oute of his londes lyinge in Bymbrydge Whyche Stipend A monke of the late Abbey of Quarre dyd yerly p'ceyve and take to his own use And dyd saye A masse ons in the weeke but syth the dyssoluc'on of the said late Abbey ther hath ben no masse ther saide or songe.

The said ffree Chaple ys scytuate and Edjfied wt. in the p'ishe of Bymbrydge dystaunt myle frome the p'ishe Churche.

The yerely Stipend unto the same Chaple belonginge by yere xls. Whyche ys wyttholden by the heyres of the said Gylbert as yt ys Thought. Ornaments plate Juell goodes Catalls merly App'teynynge or belongynge unto the sayd ffree Chapell ther ar none as ys said by the said p'isshen's."

Even earlier documentation, which predates the Domesday Book, shows Wolverton, or Ulwartone, as follows: "The King holds Ulwartone and Eddeva held it for Earl Godwin. It was then assessed at half a hide, but now at nothing. Here is 1 ploughland in demesne, with three borderers and 1 servant. It was and is worth 10s." There are also local but not positively recognized Domesday references to Hardlei and Orham (both possibly Bembridge), the latter meaning 'the settlement by the shore'. But unfortunately for the reliability or otherwise of the historical record, the Island has long boasted no less than three Wolvertons and Domesday references are almost certainly to one at Shorwell; the third is at St Lawrence.

Some of the earliest references to Wolverton date from when the Isle of Bembridge was divided into three manors of Wolverton, La Wode and Middleton. The Clamorgans, a Somerset family, owned the first two and much else besides. Peter de Clamorgan died childless, having settled the manor of Wolverton on his wife, Amice. She then married Thomas Hacket who became the guardian of Peter's brother Nicholas, "an idiot of unsound mind", and when Nicholas died in 1362 many Clamorgan estates, including Wolverton, passed to his eight sisters. Next, Thomas Hacket bought out the interests of each sister in Wolverton and settled there with his family. It eventually passed to Richard Worsley of Appuldurcombe who, through his grandmother, Joan Hacket, was descended from a junior line of the Hackets of Wolverton.

The manor at nearby Yaverland was from a very early time owned by the Russell family. Indeed, in the 13th century William Russell built the causeway and bridge that linked Yaverland to Brading, and thus the name Bembridge is derived from Binbridge ('the land within the bridge'). A well-organized Militia was ordered in 1337 and the onus of this was put on Sir Theobald Russell, Lord of Yaverland; and when, three years later, the French raided the Isle of Wight, landing at St Helens, it was Sir Theobald's men who drove the invaders back to their ships. He himself was killed in the fight.

It was this invasion, and myths which became associated with it, which inspired Ernest du Boulay more than five centuries later to weave together colourful legends about the Hermit of Culver Cliff – and about how Wolverton was razed to the ground in 1340, never to be rebuilt. One account, popular in the immediate locality today, tells how an old man, shabbily dressed, used to visit Wolverton with the purpose of selling small trinkets. He would also help the people with their domestic problems and, after following the old man's advice, they would find their troubles solved. He used to leave Wolverton in the early evening and instead of heading towards the village of Brading used to walk up to the path towards Culver Cliff. The superstitious peasants were loath to follow him. Now, at the time that the Hermit, as he was known, was carrying out his good works in the hamlet, apparently bad fortune fell on others. The Hermit explained that a stranger dressed in a grey cowl was responsible for this and described the man in some detail, adding that in the near future the grey clad figure would be arriving at Wolverton to poison the water in the holy well.

This well was nothing more than a hole in the ground, but close by was a plain stone column, the remains of a cross, and upon the stone were engraved the following lines:

While the Oose flows pure and free,
Burg and tune shall happy bee,
The net bee heavy in the sea,
And wheaten seed shall yield plentie

When sained blood in the burn shall well
It shall light a flame so hot and snell
Shall fire the burg from lock to fell
Nor sheeling bide its place to tell
And Culvert's Nass shall ring its Knell

By the side of the well the people who had been dogged by bad luck awaited the instigator of their misfortune and before too long a very old figure, dressed as the Hermit had described, made his way towards the well. There he stood, uttering some sounds before leaning over the brink. People in the crowd, certain that he was about to poison the water, threw stones at him, until the dead body of the old stranger lay dripping blood from a head wound into the holy well.

A wise old man who witnessed the attack was too late to inform the unruly crowd that their

The copse where once a hamlet thrived and St Urian's chapel stood.

45

victim was in fact a most holy man who knew the secret properties of the well, and was by no means the source of their misfortunes. Upon hearing this revelation, the amazed crowd then realized what they had done – and the implications of the verses on the cross.

True to the engraved words, the hamlet was razed to the ground by the French during the battle in which Sir Theobald Russell was killed. Although the French eventually retreated to their ships, Wolverton was left a burning ruin with many of the inhabitants killed. The survivors never returned to rebuild their houses and the land was left as it was.

Over six hundred years have passed since that day, and Islanders prefer to believe the legend that is attached to the spot, thanks to du Boulay, than to accept the dull historical fact that the French were easily repulsed.

Many local people believe that the wood is haunted by the unfortunate holy man in the grey cowl. Undoubtedly Centurion's Copse has a curious feeling about it. Some say that their dogs will not walk in Pilgrim's Lane after twilight. Without question there is a strange lack of bird song in the wood. However, what is certain is that this small, seemingly insignificant area of woodland has inspired some of the more unusual tales of the Isle of Wight.

Overners - An Anthropological Survey
REGGIE BENNETT

The species Man is divided into two sub-species: Islanders and Overners. This distinction existed far back in history, indeed in pre-history for all I know. It is a clear one, well understood by those in either category. And although the Overner may consider himself an islander of sorts, living in an island as he does, that does not count. To those poor folk whose lot it is to live in continental Europe the Englishman may seem to be an islander; this is just a foreign delusion. The Englishman is an Englishman, *tout court*. The only real Islander is, and has always been, an autochthonous denizen of the Isle of Wight.

This matter has not concerned anybody very much for most of the millennia since Mankind evolved and populated the planet. It can only have been a minuscule affair so long as the communications between the Isle of Wight and the coasts opposite were restricted to the dug-out canoe, the coracle, or even the earliest forms of sailing hoy. It was with the invention of steam engines and the rapid development of transport, especially by sea, that the contented and undisturbed natives were made aware of England opposite and its large population.

Then began the seasonal migrations, like those of the world of birds, between the great industrial cities of England and the Isle of Wight. Almost incomprehensible differences of speech marked permanently the difference between otherwise indistinguishable individuals; but in time the social mores and dietetic quirks of the invaders, who were peaceable enough, tended to be adopted increasingly by the Islanders. These showed a readiness to trade, and soon found it rewarding to provide food, lodging or transport – for a handsome consideration. And in this way they learned to limit the time-scale, at least, of the migrations. One week or two sufficed to empty the pockets of the Overners and they would return, lightened and refreshed, to England, their mainland.

In the present century these migrations became massive, and indeed many may still remember the tightly-packed masses, eight deep, who occupied the length of the embarkation piers on either coast, patiently waiting in the gales and rain of the northern summer, for space in the steam ferries. More recently they have, as in the dawn of history, developed into the equivalent of the centaur, part man and part vehicle; these hybrids now crowd across on a larger and different type of vessel. Their mobility has increased and they are everywhere – though still not for long. They come, and they go – empty handed. And the Islander smiles either way.

It has only been in most recent times that previously regular migrants began to settle in the Island later in life. Even then they remained Overners, with their own peculiar ways, and generally confined themselves to enclaves of their own kind. The Islanders tolerated them kindly, continued to thrive upon them – but remained a genus apart.

A race apart ... the true Islander.

(Patrick Eden/Island Life)

So how do we tell these two sub-species from each other? It is by no means easy, for physical differences are few. Both are crouching, waddling anthropoids of something like pre-Cromagnon build. Their metabolism is similar, as indigenous habits have yielded to the customs of the migrants; it has been said that the latter outnumber the former by several hundred per cent during the migratory season. For instance, a particularly near-universal tropism, the well-known Terramalacomminutaphilia* has almost smothered many of the simple reflexes of the native population and is almost certainly derived from the society of the Overner.

Even in speech, so often a guide to tribal origins, this mutual incomprehensibility (while still proclaiming the same formal tongue) has yielded slightly. In respect of the populations immediately facing each other across the tide-torn and usually escape-proof waters that separate them there is some common ground. The denizens of territories within visual distance of the Island have developed diphthongs which only the highest linguistic scholars could distinguish from those of the Island population. From any territories further afield than the nearer shores of Wessex, however, the glottal stops, the shortened vowels, altered phonemes and other traits make identification easy.

So much for anthropology – a dismal enough science second only to economics. Linguistics, too, that nit-picking art, can bog us down indefinitely, as you have seen. Then how *do* we spot them?

He is a brave man who would nominate any sure shibboleth. I flinch from that. But there is one simple test which, having bred two Overners and two Islanders, I think I dare put before the reader. It is this:

Lead the person under examination into discussion about the actual crossing of the water-barrier. With some care, and sufficient skill, the investigator can lead the 'interviewee' into referring to this crossing. A reference to a crossing "over to England" reveals the true Islander. This test is virtually definitive. The Overner, or Englander, would never say that.

We have now seen that our two sub-species can usually be identified, and that in spite of long exposure to each other they can preserve their identity indefinitely. But how about miscegenation?

*"chips with everything"

Well, there is clearly no bar to cross-fertilization, and there is obviously a good deal of it about. In such cases the progeny will most probably follow the dominant ethos of their early environment. If reared on the Island they will condition easily into Islanders. If their upbringing is that of an Overner, Overners they will become to all external appearances. However they may at any time succumb to an atavism and 'go native', when the underlying Island strain asserts itself. It is always there, and in its most rudimentary form may amount to nothing more than a tendency to scrutinize the number-plates of cars, looking for the letters DL. A harmless trait, revealing nothing more than a rather touching nostalgia deriving from a deep-lying archetype.

But is a change possible, among otherwise confirmed Overners or Islanders? It is hard to say. This, too, must depend largely on the environmental influences at work during a lifetime. I myself really do not know at what point an Overner evolves into an Islander; I am quite certain, however, that an Islander never becomes an Overner. I suppose that my own case may serve to add some confusion to an already muddled situation.

Having frequented the Island myself for some 60 years in all, I could not on that account claim to be an Islander. Obviously not. But I had a house – a series of houses – or houseboats for a quarter of a century during that time and bred some Islander offspring. After so many years I certainly became Islander-orientated, to say the least. And now I'm an Overner again.

This sort of thing gives one a severe attack of split personality. For instance, I sat in Parliament for Fareham for some 30 of those years, so that I saw the Island as an Overner would. I would hear a respected constituent say: "Them people over there, in that there Island, d'ye know they still go about on all fours? Know why? Nobody's told them what their hands are for." And then when I'd been living in the East Medine for a while, one of the local fellows there confided to me: "You know them Overners over there in Fareham?" "Yes, indeed I do." "Well, did you know that when an organ-grinder turned up there with his monkey, they all believed the monkey was one of them French prisoners-of-war." The compliments still fly.

One such compliment, addressed to the Island population, is to refer to them as 'corkheads' or 'caulkheads'. No doubt this is intended to imply

48

that they are thick, or solid between the ears, even if both spellings seem to suffer an ability to remain afloat individually. I know not whether such a meaning, or any other meaning, is widely accepted. It would seem, however, that this particular compliment dates far back before the invention of writing and spelling – for both versions sound alike.

Now, in this long and, I fear, excessively pedantic anthropological treatise I have so far omitted reference to one group of inmates of the Island who may well defy classification. In the West Medine there are a number of large guest-houses and camps, well-built and very well staffed, to which Overners come for longer than the conventional week or two. Indeed, they may live in the Island for longer than some of the settlers mentioned above.

Long as they may live here, and closely as they may resemble some of the real Islanders, they are never assimilated. After a period of some years they leave the Island without any apparent regret – indeed, some may have tried to wrench themselves away sooner, but have failed. They revert to being unrepentant Overners, and their idyllically named places of residence may see them no more – not if they can help it. We cannot, and would not, claim these as Islanders, any more than they would claim it themselves.

These, then, are in my view the various categories of Islanders and Overners and their relationships. It is an uneasy symbiosis, but it endures. Kindness to Overners is a philanthropic movement which has been, perhaps, unusually slow to develop – but in this beautiful Island there is, as usual, no hurry. Long may this be so!

Optimists at Bembridge Harbour ... from the original water-colour by local artist Cavendish Morton.

(*Cavendish Morton*)

J. Howard Whitehouse and the Ruskin Galleries at Bembridge School

JAMES S. DEARDEN

In 1914 J. Howard Whitehouse, Member of Parliament for Mid-Lanark, bought two small fields on the top of the cliffs overlooking Whitecliff Bay near Bembridge. They were intended as a permanent site for the Secondary School Boys Camp which Whitehouse ran for several weeks every summer. In the following year, Whitecliff Bay House, immediately adjacent to one of the fields, came on the market, and Whitehouse was able to buy this too.

In the rearrangement of constituencies which preceded the 1919 parliamentary election, Mid-Lanark disappeared and Whitehouse contested and lost neighbouring Hamilton. Thus at the age of 46 he was free to embark on a new career. He had always been fascinated by youth and education, and he determined to found and run a school where he could put into practice his educational theories, many of them advanced for their time.

His property at Bembridge provided the nucleus of a site for his educational experiment and it was here in May 1919 that Bembridge School began. Whitehouse's theories of the importance of creative education had been derived from his reading of the works of John Ruskin, and Whitehouse brought with him to Bembridge the collection of Ruskin books and drawings which he had already been assembling for twenty years.

Whitehouse was born in Birmingham in 1873. He began his working life with Cadbury Brothers at Bournville and continued his education by attending evening classes at Mason's College. Here he was introduced to the writings and teaching of John Ruskin. Whitehouse was a great organizer and never came into contact with new ideas without doing something about them. His interest in Ruskin inspired him in 1896 to found the Ruskin Society of Birmingham - just one of a half dozen similar societies in the country at that time. Such lecturers as Dean Farrar, F.J. Furnivall, Sir Michael Sadler, Canon Rawnsley and Sir Oliver Lodge were persuaded by Whitehouse to address meetings of the society, which soon grew in membership to over 500.

John Ruskin's 80th birthday in 1899 brought

John Ruskin's photograph and signature.

(Roger Sawyer)

the usual Victorian influx of illuminated addresses; the address sponsored by the Ruskin Society of Glasgow was subscribed to by most of the other parallel societies and allied organizations which were inspired by The Master's teaching. The address was borne to Coniston by Whitehouse and the secretary of the Liverpool society. We can read of the visit in Whitehouse's diary:

7 Feb 1899. To Coniston to bear to Mr Ruskin the National Address of congratulation promoted by the Ruskin Societies. I left Birmingham at 9 o'clock and reached Coniston

at 4. I put up at the Dove Hotel and after tea I drove to Brantwood to arrange time of presenting the address on the morrow ...

8 Feb. The morning was fairly bright and clear and at 11 o'clock we started for Brantwood where we were politely received by Mr & Mrs Arthur Severn. They explained that the Master felt equal to receiving us... We were then conducted to Mr Ruskin's presence. He was dressed and sitting in an arm chair before a little table. As we entered he attempted to rise, but was evidently too feeble to do so. We shook hands and I told him I was glad to hear he was so well. I then explained that we brought him a national address, and I read it to him. After he had looked at the address ... he dictated to Mrs Severn a reply ... What most impressed me when I saw the Master were his wonderful eyes. They are blue and very clear and bright. When, during the reading of the address, I looked up at him, I found them fixed upon me as though he were searching me through and through ...

This was the only occasion on which Whitehouse met Ruskin; he next visited Coniston in the following January to attend the Master's funeral.

Nothing was more natural for Whitehouse, who was a collector at heart, than to collect Ruskin's works. Whenever the opportunity arose he would buy one of the Master's books, or letters, or pictures. After Ruskin's death, Brantwood was inherited by Arthur and Joan Severn. They proceeded, over the next quarter of a century, to break up the collection there - and Whitehouse was a willing buyer. By 1919, the centenary of Ruskin's birth, he had acquired quite an interesting collection and in this year he not only founded a school but was also instrumental in forming the Ruskin Centenary Council which held an exhibition and lectures at Burlington House in the autumn.

By 1929 Whitehouse's Ruskin collection had outgrown the confines of his study and he started to build two galleries as an extension to the New House, recently designed for him by Baillie Scott. The galleries were intended not only to house his collection but also to be beautiful rooms, beautifully furnished with fine things where boys could enjoy the appreciation of first class design and workmanship. The galleries were formally opened on 19th November 1930 by Albert Rutherston, Master of the Ruskin Drawing School at Oxford. In the course of his address Rutherston said:

... Your Warden Whitehouse has been inspired by far greater ideals than merely building these rooms. These rooms are the outcome of a life-long love of things spiritual and things belonging to the arts. He began to collect the contents of these rooms many years ago, and when the occasion comes they are furnished in a manner worthy of their architecture ...

The Brantwood dispersal sales of 1930-31 provided Whitehouse with further opportunity to enlarge his collection. In 1932 he bought Brantwood itself. Today, Brantwood is open to the public so that they may see its large collection of pictures, books and Ruskin furniture. Additions were made to the Bembridge collection whenever possible, though the actual ownership of the collection had been handed over to the Education Trust, established by Whitehouse to accept financial responsibility for Bembridge School. Today the collection of Ruskin's pictures, letters, manuscripts and books at Bembridge is unequalled in the world and the galleries are frequently visited by international scholars engaged in research.

The galleries themselves comprise two rooms, each measuring 39 feet by 21 feet. The lower gallery, now called The Warden's Library, is furnished as a library containing an extensive and comprehensive collection of books by Ruskin, together with many volumes formerly in the Brantwood library. The ever-growing number of books about Ruskin has outgrown the space available in this room and they are now housed in adjacent rooms. There are also an art section and a series of books by Whitehouse and his friends.

The walls of the staircase are lined with pictures by Ruskin's friends and contemporaries, while the upper gallery contains drawings and watercolours by Ruskin himself. Here also is kept the bulk of the manuscript collection.

To illustrate the extent of the collection some statistics may not be amiss. The galleries contain upwards of 1,400 original pictures, more than half of them by Ruskin; some 6,500 letters, of

Interior of the Ruskin Galleries at Bembridge School.

(James S. Dearden/ Ruskin Galleries)

which about 5,000 are written by Ruskin; 114 complete or fragmentary literary manuscripts; 466 books from the library at Brantwood, with over 125 other associated or inscribed volumes. There are, in addition, copies of most of the books and articles about Ruskin and an almost complete collection of the many different editions of his works.

From time to time pictures or other items in the collection may be moved temporarily to Brantwood, to be replaced by ones brought south from there. There are also frequent and substantial loans to exhibitions. In recent years items from the collection have been seen in many galleries in this country, and in America, Italy and Switzerland.

Ruskin's eminence as a writer has rather overshadowed his work as an artist; but during his lifetime he made an enormous number of sketches and drawings. Many were made as a person today would take photographs - in order to remember scenes or details which caught his attention, or to illustrate a particular point which he was discussing in his books or lectures. This partly explains why so many of his drawings appear to be unfinished - they were never intended to be complete pictures, but simply notes in graphic form - albeit very beautiful notes. Another reason why Ruskin drew was to learn by copying - in the case of one of the earliest drawings in the collection, made in 1826-7 at the age of eight or nine and inscribed later in life "My first map of Italy", he wanted to remember details of the country. When he was ten or eleven he used his first sketchbook, now at Bembridge, and in it drew "My first tree from nature, 1831", "Gateway of a college at Maidstone", corners of Dover and Tonbridge Castles, and the main tower of Canterbury Cathedral. Among the earliest finished pencil drawings are his very stylised Dover Castle, and Battle Abbey.

By 1835 (aet 16), the year of his first important continental tour, he was making large numbers of pencil drawings. His architectural studies were based on the style of Samuel Prout, while his landscapes were based on engravings after the work of J.M.W.Turner, whom he greatly admired. This phase is represented in the collection by "Calais from the sea", "Street scene in Berne", "Church of S.Anastasia, Verona", and many others. Two copies after Prout's Hotels des villes at Brussels and Louvain, drawn about this time, are fine pieces of work. The two British tours of 1837-8 produced another well-represented crop of drawings, in which his own mannerisms begin to emerge. In the early 1840s he came under the influence of David Roberts's work, a style reflected in "Old Houses at Rouen" and the "Trevi Fountain at Rome".

The year 1842 saw Ruskin's realization that copying and imitating other people's styles did not constitute *seeing* nature and drawing what was really there. Henceforward he began a series of studies from Nature, and the development of his own style is clearly evident in such drawings as "Mountain rock and alpine rose" (1844), "Venice: Ca'd'Oro" (1845), and "Mountains of Villeneuve" (1846), engraved for *Modern Painters*. The collection contains a mass of sketches and notes made in the 1850s for *Stones of Venice*, which illustrate how clearly Ruskin saw what he drew. "The Walls of Lucerne" (1854), with its apparently disconnected pockets of detail, is a fine picture; the 1862 "View from the base of the Brezon above Bonneville, looking towards Geneva" has a remarkable three-dimensional effect.

Among Ruskin's copies from the Old Masters are Tintoretto's "Adoration of the Magi", and "Crucifixion" (he did much to bring Tintoretto and the early Italian masters to the notice of the British public), parts of Veronese's "Cuccina Family" and the charming group of roses from the dress of Spring in Botticelli's "Primavera", which was later engraved and used as a vignette on the title pages and covers of many of his books.

Drawings of Venice and Verona are well represented in the collection. There are also many charming and fine studies of minerals, birds, flowers and trees. Another treasure is Ruskin's last sketchbook, with one of his last drawings - "Langdale Pikes" (1889).

The work of Ruskin's artist friends and protégés is represented in examples by Millais, Albert Goodwin, Laurence Hilliard, W.G. Collingwood, Fairfax Murray, T. M. Rooke, Stacy Marks, Isabella Jay, Edward Burne-Jones, W. H. Hunt, Samuel Prout, the Severns (Joseph, Arthur and Walter), David Roberts, and others. Here too are six bird drawings by Thomas Bewick, formerly in Ruskin's collection, George Richmond's striking portrait of John James Ruskin, and a dozen portraits of Ruskin himself.

Perhaps the most important items in the manuscript collection are the 29 volumes of Ruskin's Diary - all-important in their original form to scholars and biographers. Here are also notebooks, manuscripts and corrected proofs of Ruskin's books: *Stones of Venice, Modern Painters, Love's Meinie, Notes on Turner's Drawings, Bible of Amiens, Fors Clavigera*, and some fragments of the manuscript of his auto-biography, *Praeterita*. A valuable source of biographical material is contained in Ruskin's father's Account Books (1827-1863) and Diaries (1833-64), with their faltering notes made a few days before his death.

The wealth of the letter collection lies in the family correspondence. There are 84 letters from Ruskin's father to his wife, and almost twice as many in reply, many containing notes and poems to his father written by the young John. One of these includes his "first" letter, copied from the childish scrawl by Margaret Ruskin and signed by John himself. Here are 267 letters to Ruskin from his father and 395 from Ruskin to his mother. John James's activities as a successful sherry importer are graphically illustrated by the file of correspondence with his partner Pedro Domecq. J.J.R.'s last two letters, business letters written just a few days before his death and described in *Praeterita,* are in the collection. But perhaps the most biographically important series of letters is that written by Ruskin to his cousin and adopted daughter, Joan Severn - some 2,900 letters written between 1864 and 1895.

Much of Ruskin's early literary work was edited by W.H. Harrison; here is a long series of letters to him from father and son. Ruskin's later policy of attending to his own printing and publishing is represented by over 200 letters to George Allen, his publisher, and Henry Jowett, manager of Hazell, Watson and Viney's printing works. Whitehouse was able to bring together an enormous collection of letters which are now invaluable to the Ruskin scholar.

There is little of bibliographical interest in the

collection of books from Brantwood. Most of their value lies in their association interest and in the copious notes and sketches made in them by Ruskin. There are several family bibles and prayer books. A number of the volumes were his father's: Reichard's *Itinerary of Italy*, used and annotated on their journeys, the *Architectural Magazine* containing John's first serious articles on "The Poetry of Architecture", for example. Ruskin's own books include Cuvier's *Natural History*, Bekker's Plato, with the *Laws* annotated, several of the volumes he used at Oxford, *Friendship's Offering* (1835) containing his own poem "Salzburg". There are books on geology, travel and architecture. Incunabula are represented by an *Astronomicon* of 1485, and the *Dyalogues* of St Gregory. There is a small Italian illuminated manuscript from Ruskin's collection, and the eightieth birthday address referred to above; *Ethics of the Dust* inscribed to Swinburne, Lewis Carroll's copy of *Praeterita*, with his

signatures on the fly-leaves, and George Allen's copy of *The Seven Lamps of Architecture* with part of the original manuscript bound in.

The plaque which was rescued in 1969 when Ruskin's birthplace in London was demolished has been set into the outside wall of the galleries, and sometimes visitors who have not read the accompanying explanatory tablet exclaim that they didn't know Ruskin was born here! He wasn't. Despite the fact that he did visit the Island for a couple of days when he was nine years old, he did not come to Bembridge. The connection between Ruskin and Bembridge is through Whitehouse.

When Whitehouse bought his first two fields at Bembridge his purchase was to lead to the establishment here of a small but internationally famous gallery and library, which have become a monument to that great Victorian teacher, John Ruskin, and to his disciple, John Howard Whitehouse.

Newtown's 1699-built town hall serves no town at all.

Literary Connections with
the Isle of Wight
HUGH NOYES

Farringford ... built in 1806, first rented by Tennyson in 1853, and purchased by him, with its park and farmland, three years later.

The description of the Isle of Wight as the English Parnassus is no idle flight of fancy. For to this small island, scarcely larger than Malta, many of our most illustrious poets, artists and authors have been drawn to find inspiration from the sea, the solitude and the countryside. They have been coming here since the days of the Romans, some for just a fleeting visit, but others to remain for a lifetime. Nor have they come solely from our own country. From The United States came Longfellow, staying at Shanklin in "a lovely little thatch-roofed inn" and leaving a delightful inscription for the Shanklin fountain as a reminder of his visit:

O Traveller, stay thy weary feet;
Drink of this fountain, pure and sweet;
It flows for rich and poor the same:
Then go thy way, remembering still
The wayside well beneath the hill,
The cup of water in His name.

Another visitor from across the seas was the French writer Paul Bourget, described by Robert Louis Stevenson as an "exquisite fellow, all made of fiddle strings, scent and intelligence." On leaving the Island Bourget wrote to a friend that "I shall always have before my eyes adorable views of the countryside to comfort me – scenes of beautiful green lawns, cold blue seas and delicately grey skies".

Some of the Island's literary visitors – Lewis Carroll, who is believed to have written *The Hunting of the Snark* at Sandown, or Charles Dickens, who wrote several chapters of *David Copperfield* while staying at Winterbourne (now a hotel) in Bonchurch – arrived here by chance or for a short holiday. A gale forced Henry Fielding to land at Ryde, an event which resulted in an amusing account of his treatment at the hands of Ryde landladies. But others were searching for longer periods of rest while almost all must have been seeking the inspiration that the sea has given to so many poets through the ages. My father, Alfred Noyes, one of those who fell in love with the Isle of Wight and made it his home for life, said in his book *Orchard's Bay* (a secluded cove on the Undercliff) – "To have the sea for your boundary is to have a new picture before you every day". His home, Lisle Combe, stands on the cliffs above Orchard's Bay and from there he could look across the fields to the cliff path, where not so many years before, Keats and Swinburne had walked and been inspired by the same wild storm-tossed seas.

As my father wrote in *Orchard's Bay* about the cormorant – "And his way is no more changed than the wave's long whisper, though a world has gone to the grave."

One of his finest poems, although not one of the best known, is *Night Journey*, written for the Isle of Wight Home for the Blind in Newport in the closing years of his life when he himself was rapidly losing his sight. The three verses are inscribed in stone in the Home, beneath a bas-relief of my father by William King, a former president of the Royal Society of British Sculptors, who lived at Whitwell.

Thou who never canst err, for Thyself art the Way;
Thou whose infinite kingdom is flooded with day;
Thou whose eyes behold all, for Thyself art the Light,
Look down on us gently who journey by night.

So many are the literary associations of the Island that in a short essay it is impossible to include except in passing even some of the most exalted. This cannot be a complete anthology of Island writers. No mention is made, for instance, of the many living authors and poets who carry on the literary traditions of the Island to the present day. Among the earliest writers on the Isle of Wight was The Venerable Bede, who in the seventh century tells in his *Opera Historica* how the Roman Emperor Vespasian subdued the Island "standing nigh Britain southward". It was then known as 'Vecta'. Bede describes how Cadwalla also took the Isle of Wight, "which until that time had been wholly given up to the worshipping of idols". As far as I know, since the days of Cadwalla, Islanders have seldom reverted to the worship of idols. Indeed, some much-loved hymns – "There's a friend for little children" and "Eternal light, Eternal light" – are of Island authorship.

But while Bede may have been among the earliest writers on the Isle of Wight, few would dispute that the poet laureate, Alfred Lord Tennyson, was the most illustrious. Tennyson came to Farringford in 1853 when Freshwater was a simple fishing village and Totland did not exist. The poet laureate and his wife crossed the Solent in a rowing boat and it is said that when they first went to Farringford two of their servants burst into tears, saying that they could never live in so lonely a place. It was the solitude of Farringford, of course, that appealed to Tennyson and within a year he was writing his well-known invitation to his friend, the Rev. F. D. Maurice, to visit him in his island retreat:

Where, far from noise and smoke of town,
I watch the twilight falling brown.
All round a careless ordered garden,
Close to the ridge of a noble down.

For groves of pine on either hand,
To break the blast of Winter, stand.
And further on the hoary channel
Tumbles a breaker on chalk and sand.

Having discovered Farringford at the age of 43, he made it his principal residence until his death in 1892. Here, in his island retreat, he wrote many of his most famous poems: *Maud, The Charge of the Light Brigade, Enoch Arden, The Idylls of the King,* and in 1889, when he was 81, his well-known *Crossing the Bar*, written after a journey across the Solent from Lymington to Yarmouth.

Not always to Tennyson's liking, Farringford became a place of pilgrimage for many famous literary and political figures of the day – Swinburne, Longfellow, Oliver Wendell Holmes, the singer Jenny Lind, Charles Darwin, Garibaldi and Edward Lear. One of the more exotic visitors was Queen Emma of the Sandwich Islands for whom Tennyson had built a special throne of ilex wood, grown on the estate. Farringford remained in the ownership of the Tennyson family until after the Second World War. One of the best-loved plants in our own garden at Lisle Combe is a seedling of the famous yew at Farringford of which Tennyson wrote: "O brother, I have seen this yew tree smoke, spring after spring, for half a hundred years." Another is a young Cedar of Lebanon descended from the great cedar at Swainston which gave inspiration for another poem – "Art thou sighing for Lebanon in the long breeze that streams to thy delicious East." These were presents to my father from the grandson of the poet, a younger Alfred Tennyson.

It is all too easy to continue with endless tales of Tennyson and the Isle of Wight, but there are many poets who have written delightfully but who have not met with such public acclaim. Jean Ingelow wrote a long narrative poem describing one of the small coves along the Undercliff. Of this poem, my father wrote that her description was so accurate that the exact spot where her three characters were sitting could be indicated to within a few feet:

The Pelham woods
Were full of doves that cooed at ease;
The orchis filled her purple hoods
For dainty bees.

Another poet who spent a few of her formative years in the Isle of Wight was Alice Meynell. Writing in her diary of a ball at Steephill Castle (now a housing estate), Alice shows that a 17-year-old today is not much different from her counterpart of 100 years ago:

I wore a ravishing yellow tarlatan of the palest possible tint by night, a red rose with its leaves in my hair, and one at my waist. Off at 9.15 in time for the first quadrille. Glorious fun. Captain Sewell many times watched me going round and told Douglas how well I danced (who told me). I had no regular flirtation and no particular compliments save that truest of all, that the men quarrelled to dance with me. I would willingly have given a certain Mr Bury a dance had I been free as he very much desired it.

Alice's mother's account of another ball at Steephill Castle shows that mothers have not changed much either in the last century. "The ball was splendid", writes Mrs Thompson, "a profusion of pink lights, a flow of champagne - but poor me! - about 12 I was so utterly exhausted I had to go up into the bedroom and there lie covered up till 2.30 in a torpor. I seemed to be listening for a week to hideous gallops, waltzes etc. drumming up through the floor - Also every now and then poor Miss Johnson was brought up to be sick by her Mama."

It sounds very much like a 19th-century version of *Top of the Pops*!

Another poet of the 19th century, sadly overshadowed by Tennyson, was Sidney Dobell who came to the Island to escape the rigours of mainland winters. Dobell, however, was an exception to the rule that poets gain inspiration from the sea. Writing from Niton he says of the sea: "How I hate it! A brave man can hate nothing that there is a chance of conquering, but this blind, senseless, woman-drowning, child-freezing, man-choking god – I stand and look at it here till every drop of blood in my body is black."

Before Cobell, John Keats also visited the Island, staying at Eglantine Cottage, Shanklin, and also at Carisbrooke, where he began one of his most famous works, *Endymion*, opening with some of the best-known lines in English poetry:

A thing of beauty is a joy forever
Its loveliness increases; it will never
Pass into nothingness.

Keats made two journeys to the Island, in 1817 and 1819. Little remains now of Eglantine Cottage although a plaque on a wall of the present building, unveiled in 1956, reminds 20th-century holiday-makers of the poet's all too brief connections with the Island.

Twenty-five years earlier, in 1793, another visitor was William Wordsworth when he witnessed the British fleet preparing for sea off Portsmouth at the start of Napoleonic wars. He tells how he left with melancholy forebodings that the struggle which was about to begin and which many thought would be brought to a speedy conclusion by the irresistible arms of Great Britain would, in fact, be of long duration. It was the sight of the fleet in the Solent preparing for war that inspired a passage in *The Prelude:*

> I beheld the vessels lie,
> A brood of gallant creatures, in the deep;
> I saw them in their rest, a sojourner
> Through a whole month of calm and glassy days
> In that delightful island which protects
> Their place of convocation.

Freshwater and Farringford will always be connected with Tennyson but, moving eastwards along the southern coast of the Island to the Undercliff and beyond, the village of Bonchurch is almost as securely linked to Swinburne. And not only Swinburne, for in this tiny and picturesque corner of the Island, wonderfully protected by the mighty St Boniface Down, came many of the most eminent literary figures of the 19th century.

Among these was John Sterling, who died from consumption at an early age but who was already being acclaimed for his poetry by Tennyson, Wordsworth and Coleridge. He describes the Undercliff as it then was, in one of his poems:

> Ay, there in truth they are, the quiet homes
> And hallowed birth-spots of the English race,
> Scattered at will beneath the crag's rude face,
> While springs gush round, and near the ocean
> foams.

Sterling's burial at Bonchurch in 1844 brought together some of the most distinguished literary figures of the day. Surrounding the open grave were Tennyson, Thomas Carlyle, F.D. Maurice, Monckton Mills, Cardinal Newman's brother Francis, and many others.

A few years later in 1849, Charles Dickens came to Bonchurch and, according to the booklet

Alfred Noyes made the Island his home for life.
(Hugh Noyes)

celebrating the centenary of the Church of St Boniface there, he 'borrowed' the names of two local characters – Mr Dick for *David Copperfield* and Miss Dick for *Great Expectations.* A year later, Lord Macaulay (*Lays of Ancient Rome*) spent a working holiday at Madeira Hall, near Bonchurch, while he was writing his *History of England.*

"I look out on one side," he wrote to his friend, Thomas Ellis, "to the crags and myrtles of the Undercliff. On the other side, I have a view of the sea, which is at this moment as blue as the sky and as calm as the Serpentine".

But the poet whose name will be forever linked with Bonchurch is Algernon Charles Swinburne. His childhood and early years were spent mainly at the family home at East Dene and, although he died in his Putney home, The Pines, in 1909, his choice for a burial spot was the churchyard of St Boniface.

> Not in the cold, grey Abbey, nor where the wind sweeps cold,
> O'er the silver coat of the beech and the gorse's blazen gold,
> But there, in the isle where the gates of sea-washed England stand.

Thomas Hardy, visiting Swinburne's grave in 1910, wrote *A Singer Asleep*:

In this fair niche above the unslumbering sea,
The Fates have fitly bidden that he should be
Pillowed eternally.'

Tales of the poet's boyhood in the Isle of Wight are numerous but one of the most fascinating describes his attempt to prove his manhood by scaling the mighty Culver Cliff at Sandown. In the belief that his parents doubted his courage, he set out to prove them wrong and was nearly killed in the attempt. On reaching the top of Culver he was so exhausted that he lost consciousness, awaking to find a sheep licking his face. According to the young Swinburne, the sheep was looking at him with such pity and sympathy that he vowed never to eat mutton again.

Shortly before the family home was sold in 1865, Swinburne spent a winter in the Island when he began one of his greatest works, *Atalanta in Calydon*. Started at East Dene in 1863, it was continued in the library of North Court, the beautiful old Manor House at Shorwell, home of his aunt, Lady Gordon, and of her daughter, Mary Gordon (Mrs Disney Leith), the only woman Swinburne truly loved. The opening lines of a poem she wrote in 1910, a year after his death, tell how Swinburne's loyalty to the Isle of Wight continued throughout his life and long after the sale of East Dene:-

April that "made" and took him comes once more
To that fair Undercliff he loved so well.

In the words of the rector at the funeral service, "today Bonchurch receives into its faithful keeping and loving care a creative genius of the first order." Although not all at the graveside would have agreed, *The Times* described the ceremony as a "fitting and beautiful end to a noble and beautiful life."

My father, who, as a young poet, met Swinburne and had several lengthy discussions with him in his library at The Pines, believed that in spite of his outwardly atheistic views, Swinburne was much closer to Christianity than he would publicly admit.

So, from Cadwalla and the Venerable Bede down to the present day, the Isle of Wight has always been a cherished refuge beyond the Solent for those wishing to escape the maelstrom and false sophistication of the world. As Lord Mottistone, father of our Lord Lieutenant, says in *Fear and Be Slain*, "I have come to love very deeply these native island folk... They are different from any other people in the British Isles, and it may well take a lifetime to understand them... Although they regard all the rest of the world as 'Overners', in moments of real emergency and danger they are prepared to hazard life itself even for these despised strangers."

Through the centuries, the 'Overners' from the world of letters have been made particularly welcome, perhaps because they too, in coming here, are seeking something different from what is sought by any other people in the British Isles.

Charles Tennyson Turner and his younger brother, the poet laureate, sometimes composed poetry together in their youthful days by walking on opposite sides of a hedge and shouting to each other any particularly fancied line. It is fitting that Charles should, perhaps, sum up best the relationship between the poetic 'Overners' and the natives in his *Farewell to the Isle of Wight*:

My memory wander'd back
To those fair shores - the Needles and the Downs -
The happy woodlands and the little towns -
For every day a new and pleasant track;
How grieved was I those social walks to lose,
Those friendly hands!

Some Painters
of the Isle of Wight
PAMELA FREEMAN

It seems strange that the Isle of Wight, famous for its natural beauties, has stimulated more literary than visual, creative and artistic output. But, apart from two giant names – Turner and Ruskin (who had direct or, in the case of Ruskin, mainly indirect Island connections) – the list of Island visual artists from the 17th century to the present day, whilst including some well-known people, seems largely composed of worthy middle-rankers.

Let us start with the major artist, J.M.W. Turner. Turner was born in 1775. A water-colour of his of Alum Bay was painted in 1795, and *The Cholmeley Sea Piece,* a picture of fishermen at sea off the Needles, was the first oil painting he ever exhibited. In 1827 he visited the architect John Nash at East Cowes Castle. (Nash's elegantly designed country house at Bembridge has been ruthlessly diminished and destroyed by our latter-day vandals in their headlong rush for money.) On this visit Turner did a series of oil sketches of shipping and regattas in the Solent: interesting early records of marine activities based on the Island.

And then, George Morland (1763-1804). Poor George, a sad man whose struggle to evade the debt-collectors, and to finance his serious bouts of drinking, brought him on several occasions to seek sanctuary on the Isle of Wight. But, in spite of his inability to manage the economics of his life, he is well remembered for lovely rustic and pastoral paintings: pictures of a long-vanished countryside, and the wretched lives of its inhabitants, which became a yardstick for romantic paintings of rural England until the great beam of Constable arrived to lift this genre on to an international level.

Two excellent mid-19th-century oil paintings in the Victoria and Albert Museum, by Richard Burchett and E.W. Cooke, have become well-known from their modern use as picture-postcards: the former's grand view of Culver Cliff from the fields above Shanklin, and the latter's *Mending the Bait Net,* also painted at Shanklin, this time on the beach. Both paintings show that 19th-century confidence which reflects British ascendancy in world affairs.

Harvesting at Shanklin ... painted by Richard Burchett in 1855.

(Victoria and Albert Museum).

And George Brannon, printmaker, whose delightful series, *Sketches of Scenery in the Isle of Wight,* (1832), *Vectis Scenery,* (1841) and *Pictorial Beauties of the Isle of Wight* (also 1841), did much to popularize as a holiday resort the Island and its topography to the prosperous middle and lower middle classes. George Brett seems to be the only pre-Raphaelite to have had any first-hand connection with the Island, with a lovely water-colour called *February in the Isle of Wight* (1866).

The Church also made its contributions: two cartoonist clerics – the Rev. R. Edwards (1809), with his pen drawings of Shanklin life, and the Rev. J.L. Jefferson (1902), sketches of holidaying crowds in the then style of *Punch,* also at Shanklin, and, far more importantly, the great poet-monk, Gerard Manley Hopkins, who was doing strong and passionate drawings of Island places towards the end of the Victorian era.

It is not possible to leave the fruitful 19th century without mentioning John Ruskin. Though Ruskin was not an Islander, the Ruskin Collection housed in a purpose-built museum at Bembridge School, through the generosity of Howard Whitehouse, covers the work – drawings, paintings, notebooks and memorabilia – of one of this country's real luminaries, who took the arts, including criticism, literature and natural history, off their specialist heights, and placed them firmly in the hands of all of us.

The 20th century has produced a great wealth of interest in the fine arts, given expression by the activities of many local art societies and regularly run classes. The Technical College, the Quay Arts Centre and many schools, all giving facilities and tuition, which otherwise would be hard come by, have all helped to foster and promote this interest. Shops selling artists' materials, and galleries selling the finished works across the Island are often meeting places and centres for the exchange of ideas, which both support and spread and, along with the library service, do so much to communicate to an enthusiastic public the wealth of their artistic heritage.

It seems to me to be necessary when assessing artistic activities in the Isle of Wight to distinguish between those professionals to whom art was their living and their life's work, and the vast numbers of amateur artists who – no less important – are the grass-roots of the arts. Of the former, mention here must be made of Norman Wilkinson, a largely marine artist, but also known for his work in the 1920s on the Queen's Dolls House; of Norman Hepple, an academician and royal portraitist; and of Cavendish Morton, who is still working on the Island, and whose huge output of marine and scenic paintings captures the outdoor 'feel' and varied light of the seas and coastal landscapes of the locality. Victor Voysey was another prolific painter mainly of portraits and studio work, but also of some landscapes.

Barbara Jones is an excellent illustrator, whose delightful King Penguin book shows some of the Island whimsies and fantasies. Peter Wright's very interesting neo-abstract paintings have won him acclaim, not only on the Island but also in London. He is also a gifted teacher and as such has been responsible for many years for the furthering of art education on the Island. His (nearly) non-figurative paintings of Island scenery are fresh and lively. Frank and Pamela Freeman, also both painters and teachers, though with very differing styles, have made contributions. Frank Freeman produced some charming small paintings of sailing, as well as some very large pieces, mainly expressionist, painted before his retirement from teaching. His wife, Pamela, a minor botanical illustrator and also teacher, has, with other Island names like Paddy Kerr, Walter Sharr, Esther Rose and the Rev. R. Bowyer, managed to help some of the many enthusiastic groups which regularly meet to practise some form of the visual arts.

This short sketch of just a few of the many devotees, whose concern was or is with the image and the trained eye, may perhaps give an idea of the number who have been inspired by the small glories of our island home.

The Fort and its Walk

ROGER SAWYER

The annual walk to the fort ... from a painting by Cavendish Morton

Every year, during late July or early August when the tide is right and there is no clash with the local social calendar, a whistle is blown and about four hundred people from all walks of life and several nationalities walk through the receding tide and across the mouth of the Yar to St Helen's Fort. England being England, the weather is often frightful and yet the tradition persists. There is something especially English about 'The Walk to the Fort'; the sheer point-lessness of the activity seems to be one of its main attractions. Efforts to make it a sponsored event have always been resisted, though it is not unknown for the whistle-blower to be confronted by a child clutching an entrance fee. How did this phenomenon begin and why, as the years go by, does it attract even more lemmings?

Although one of Palmerston's 'Follies', built to discourage a French invasion, the fort was not completed until long after Lord Palmerston's death. More than a century later, when the Secretary of State for Defence was making one of several attempts to relieve the taxpayer of responsibility for maintaining this fairly massive edifice - more of a white whale than a white elephant, though by no means white - it was

described in an impressive brochure as "an Ancient Monument of elliptical structure, completed in 1879, having external diameters of 134 feet and 117 feet. Erected on the sea bed at the entrance to Bembridge Harbour, the fort is built on a ring of masonry comprising large concrete blocks with an outer skin of granite blocks, the interior of the ring being filled with clay and shingle and the whole being capped with a thick layer of concrete". It is the granite 'skin' which impresses the architecturally-minded visitor; the outer face of each vast block appears square, but lodged side by side they make up what the Minister's estate agent was pleased to call an ellipse.

The surveyor acting for the Department of the Environment, the body responsible for making the sale, went on to describe the accommodation arrangements in a basement and two upper floors. The basement consists of small storage compartments "for ammunition" and narrow passages are arranged "in and around a central core"; there is no natural lighting and this level is "subject to flooding as a result of water entering at the lower landing stage". The ground floor, as it were, has two rooms and two "small

62

chambers". The first, or top, floor has three larger rooms, "previously used for plant and barracks accommodation". The "dilapidated condition" of the interior was unconvincingly attributed to the existence of two more recent structures on the roof. "No mains services are available. Water was obtained from a deep bore in the centre of the fort, from which the submersible pump has been removed... Drainage discharges directly into the sea". The old electrical wiring was said to be in place and again the word "dilapidated" was used. The surveyor studiously avoided the word 'eerie', and well he might; nevertheless fort walkers who knew the place at the time that it came on to the market agreed that the BBC were right to use it for the filming of the series *Dr Who and the Sea-Devils*. The asking price in 1985 was "in excess of £17,000".

Despite its formidable gun emplacements and overall virtual indestructibility even in the atomic age, the fort may not have played a crucial role in saving England from the French or the Germans but, until the use of radar was perfected and indeed - as far as lesser vessels are concerned - until the present day, the flashing light which it carries has served as a valuable navigational aid. Throughout much of the fort's history it has been necessary to appoint resident caretakers and keepers of the light. In March 1926 the Langtons, a Bembridge family, were living there - husband, wife and a daughter, Ethel, aged fifteen - when a badly timed gale left the daughter stranded alone on the fort for three days, with practically no food. When supplies had nearly run out the parents had used a too brief lull in the storm to go and replenish the stores. To make matters worse, shortly before this a ship coming out of Bembridge Harbour had dragged and broken the telephone line; so the fate of shipping depended upon the girl's initiative and bravery. She had to climb the exposed ladder, over which the waves sometimes broke, and keep the light burning. This she did until rescued, despite the difficulty of opening the metal door to get into the lamp room, and of winding the mechanism when weakened by hunger. The Committee of Lloyd's of London awarded her their Meritorious Medal in bronze.

Some fifteen years later the fort was a link in the chain of naval and air defences; but soon after the war it fell into disuse as far as everything except the light was concerned, and that had become automated. Then, once again, a use was found for it, albeit for only an hour or two each year. Rather like the Olympic Games the post-war practice of walking to the fort is, according to some authorities, a revival of an older tradition. In the good old days when the beach huts extended from the Garland Club to Under Tyne, bold or bored nannies would take their charges across the sand when the tide was unusually low and look for prawns in new pools. So when, in the sixties, John Gunston, Catherine and Keith McMahon and Charles and Rupert Sawyer, with or without Nanny Gunston, became compulsive fort walkers, apparently they were revivalists, not founders.

Despite the loss of most of the huts, some of which were swept away in storms, old families continued to favour Ducie Beach and they were joined by new ones attracted by the absence of candy floss and transistors. Soon parents were bitten by the fort walking bug, but having done it once, and having satisfied one's curiosity, why go again? The children never seemed to tire of the expedition, but adults needed something more. The McMahons and the Sawyers therefore decided to choose an annual date when the walk could happen in the evening and be followed by a barbecue. At first this was on a purely personal invitation basis; friends were telephoned and that was that. When attendance had exceeded about a hundred and complete strangers had begun to wander into the crowd, load up with bottles of wine and disappear, all the hosts could do was shrug it off; but when unknown and unaccompanied children, sometimes similarly laden, struck out for the fort as the tide was coming in, it was felt that before a tragedy occurred, a few safety precautions would have to be imposed. For this reason no longer is it a twin-hosted party; now there are many self-contained groups within one wider fraternity.

The only centralized aspects of the walk are the choosing of the date and time, and the whistle blowing - though printed safety rules are displayed in Bembridge Sailing Club (first edition copies, printed by the Yellowsands Press of Bembridge School, are collectors' items). As was only fitting the first of the new-style proliferated walks was heralded by a blast on the solid gold whistle which may be found suspended from the neck of Ann Pilcher, one of the keenest fort walkers. Some holiday-makers had obviously seen the walk as a handy way of disposing of surplus children; so rule number one is "An adult *must* accompany the child or children of each family group" and parents are told to carry their children through the river, rather than abandon them at the first sight of a bottle of Scotch. On one occasion walkers on their way to the fort looked back to discover that the shore had disappeared altogether in the mist; so a second blast on the whistle always means go straight back to the beach.

Members of Trinity House and HM Coastguard were consulted when the safety rules were being drawn up. Their reaction to a mass of people walking out to sea to fulfil no useful purpose might well have been hostile. In fact it was agreed that as hitherto countless stray walkers had been tempting providence on almost every night of the season, particularly in foul weather and darkness, it would be something of a relief if people were to get the urge out of their system on one carefully chosen date. Eventually a second edition of the rules was printed, to take into account David Negus's advice about the safest way to cross the Yar; both editions were illustrated by his wife, Anne.

In 1984 *The Mail on Sunday* saw fit to mention the event: "The closest fort had been, at low tide, the recent target of nothing more dangerous than the Bembridge children's 'Fort Walk', which ends in a merry barbecue along the dusty beach", which is a fair enough summary, except that the walk is very much a jollification for the family as a whole. In 1987, as the four hundredth walker (Lieutenant-Commander Webb always counts them out and counts them back) reached the fort, the number, including as usual several MPs and members of the upper house, plus - a welcome

addition - a cavalry contingent, a small boat was seen to arrive from Seaview. The occupant politely enquired why all these men, women and children were entering his property. There was a tense moment. Previous rumours of a sale had proved false, but at least one of the printed rules stated categorically "There is no right of entry into the Fort!" and a copy was hastily produced. Fortunately everything was resolved amicably and in 1988 a record number of walkers circumnavigated the lower parapet before returning to the bonfires.

Usually walkers set off at 6.30 p.m., and within an hour the bonfires extend from the harbour to Under Tyne. As darkness falls even the polygamous tendencies of certain residents of Bembridge can be accommodated - the record holder in this respect has become part of the mythology of the walk, with a past wife, a present wife and a potential wife all at different bonfires, none knowing of the presence of the others. Certainly as the evening develops the atmosphere becomes convivial, even magical, and there is something of a climax when big fires are built even higher, partly to withstand erosion by the incoming tide. After midnight things calm down a little and the light on the fort reminds some of the one that hypnotized Gatsby: "his dream must have seemed so close that he could hardly fail to grasp it". Thanks to Cavendish Morton, who faithfully records the Fort Walk every year in his beautiful paintings, some - even, or especially, those who can scarcely put one foot in front of another - can grasp their dream. And if they miss an opportunity there is always next year. Or is there?

The Victorian Fortifications
of the Isle of Wight
ANTHONY CANTWELL AND PETER SPRACK

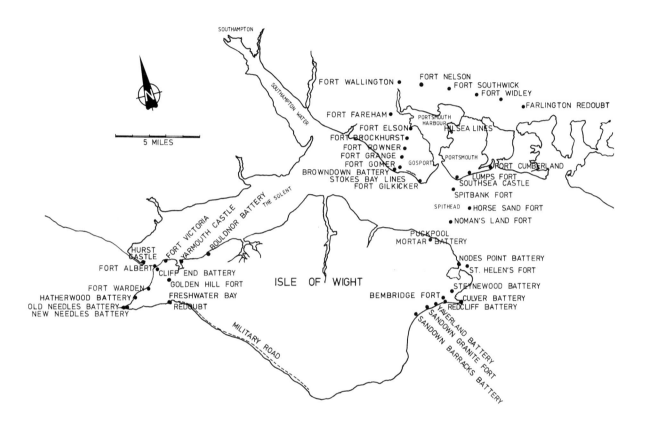

The Portsmouth Fortress and the defences of the Isle of Wight in 1870.   (Anthony Cantwell)

At first sight, the long century between the defeat of Napoleon in 1815 and the outbreak of the Great War in 1914 saw the end the old enmity with France and the evolution of a new one with Germany. After Waterloo, when British and French soldiers appeared on the same battlefield they did so as allies.

Yet appearances can be deceptive. In reality, the century witnessed a continuing rivalry between Britain and France that was characterized by what we would call an 'arms race' between the two countries. Indeed, as late as 1898, Britain and France nearly went to war over the Sudan while we were negotiating (unsuccessfully) with Germany for an alliance.

Political instability and revolution weakened France throughout the 19th century but paradoxically this only increased the apprehension in Britain of both government and people. "The modern history of France is the substitution of one crisis for another" was how Sir Robert Peel expressed it in 1849. Many French generals and admirals hoped that the introduction of new types of weapons and ships would give France political superiority at the very least. Thus France pioneered the building of steam-driven warships armed with smooth-bore guns that fired an explosive spherical shell as well as the conventional iron round shot. Yet, whatever France invented, Britain soon followed suit and usually outproduced her rival.

The attitude of the British public and their elected representatives to paying for defence oscillated according to the political situation. Usually, there was resentment at voting large sums for rearmament, succeeded overnight by demands for the government to defend the coasts whenever an invasion was feared. The Navy was the first line of defence, partly because it was rather fancifully imagined that French steamships could land thousands of men on our south coast beaches before we could mobilize, and partly because so much of our regular army was tied down in colonial defence.

Then in 1851 Louis Napoleon Bonaparte (nephew of the 'Corsican ogre') seized power in France. British fear and xenophobia ran riot and Parliament voted money for emergency defence construction. The 'crisis' passed, and soon Britain and France were allied against Russia during the Crimean War (1854-56). The foreign ambitions of the Emperor Napoleon III (as Bonaparte had proclaimed himself in 1852) caused tension in Europe and led to the 'panic' of 1859.

Three independent factors caused this particular invasion scare to have a greater influence on the state of Britain's defences than any previous one. The first was France's brief but aggressive war with Austria in Italy. The second was the launching by France of *La Gloire*, the first sea-going warship in history to be armoured with wrought-iron plates. A fleet of French 'ironclads' might overwhelm our wooden-hulled battleships, especially as the new French naval base at Cherbourg was only fifty miles from our main naval base at Portsmouth. The third was the introduction in several countries of the rifled breech-loading gun.

For over three hundred years artillery had been muzzle-loading, i.e. the propellant cartridge and the roundshot had been rammed into the open end of the gun barrel nearest the enemy. The rear (or 'breech') of the barrel was solid, in order to contain the force of the exploding gunpowder charge. In 1854, however, William (later Lord) Armstrong invented a gun with an opening breech. For the first time the inside of the barrel (the 'bore') was 'rifled' along its long axis with shallow grooves which spun an elongated, pointed shell as it was fired. Whereas the old cannon balls had tumbled erratically

through the air, the new elongated shells were far more accurate.

The Armstrong guns entered British service in 1859, the year of the invasion scare. Lord Palmerston's administration responded by appointing a Royal Commission to look at the state of Britain's defences. Its report in 1860 revealed that many coast defence works were obsolete and suggested a two-fold remedy. Britain would have her own steam ironclads of the 'Warrior' class to dispute control of the Channel. Coast defence was largely to be concentrated on protecting naval dockyards like Portsmouth and Plymouth so our fleet would have secure bases in which to effect repairs and take on ammunition and coal.

Nearly £12 million (subsequently much reduced by Parliament) was allocated to coast defence, of which £2,400,000 was to be devoted to Portsmouth and the Isle of Wight. Although that sum was soon reduced to £1,920,000 by abandoning some proposed works, Portsmouth was protected by six land forts on Portsdown Hill, against attack by invaders who might land near Chichester, advance overland and bombard the dockyard from the north. An older line of five forts, begun in 1852 west of Gosport to prevent a land advance from the west, was completed and new coast batteries built to defend the harbour.

The Isle of Wight's role in the defence of Portsmouth has been a crucial one ever since the invention of artillery. The Island acts as the stopper of the bottle which is Southampton Water, its guns helping to defend the direct approach to Portsmouth across Spithead and via the Needles Passage from the west. By the time of the Napoleonic Wars (1793-1815) coast defence was still largely provided by stone forts which Henry VIII had built in the 1540s - Southsea Castle to defend Portsmouth, Hurst and Yarmouth Castles to bar the Needles Passage, and Calshot Castle to defend Southampton Water.. To prevent an enemy landing on the Isle of Wight there was also Sandown Fort (constructed 1632-36). Earthen emergency batteries were also thrown up in the 1790s at both ends of the Island.

As a result of the 1851 scare the Tudor Hurst Castle was strengthened in 1851-56 and two new brick forts (Fort Victoria, 1855 and Fort Albert, 1856) were erected on the Isle of Wight. These covered the Needles Passage at its narrowest point, while a small fort at Freshwater Bay (Freshwater Redoubt, 1856) would prevent the

French landing there to take Forts Victoria and Albert from the landward side. The advent of the breech-loaders made the 1850s forts obsolete within a decade for their shells would have driven deep into the brick before exploding.

The new weapons meant new solutions. No guns were available with enough range to cover the whole width of Spithead. Following a proposal first mooted in 1852, three sea forts (Spit Bank, No Man's and Horse Sand) were erected on shoals to dominate the ship channel. Pre-cut granite blocks were laid in the sea bed to above high water mark and a superstructure wholly or partly of iron plate bolted to this circular foundation to protect the guns. A fourth smaller sea fort at St Helens was added later to protect that anchorage and the entrance to Brading Harbour.

The sea forts were supported by a battery at Puckpool near Ryde for 30 iron 13-inch mortars. They were placed on wooden beds at an angle of 45 degrees, range being varied by altering the powder charge. The bed was fixed to a turntable resting on timber baulks so that the weapon could be 'traversed' through 360 degrees by gunners, using metal-shod handspikes.

A major concern was that the French would land in Sandown Bay and take Puckpool Battery from the rear. Accordingly, the Sandown beaches were defended by three batteries and a fort. On the low cliffs north of the bay were Redcliff Battery (four guns) and Yaverland Battery (eight guns), with Sandown Barracks Battery (five guns) similarly placed to the south of the town. Crossfire from the three covered the beaches against landing parties. Sandown Granite Fort (now the zoo) was situated on low ground to oppose ships. Originally planned for 28 guns, the twelve eventually emplaced were located in granite-fronted brick chambers ('casemates') with wrought-iron armour shields. This gave them greater protection against fire from ironclads.

The landward defences of all these works were relatively simple: a dry ditch, brick walls loop-holed for musketry, and small blockhouses called caponiers which projected from the walls so the defenders could fire down the length of the ditch. A hexagonal land fort with wide brick-lined ditches and three double-storeyed caponiers was built on Bembridge Down to support the Sandown Bay defences. It mounted a further six guns on its ramparts which would have assisted its garrison in repelling a landing in either Sandown or Whitecliff Bays.

A hostile coast with razor-sharp offshore reefs protected the southern beaches of the Island from invaders. Despite plans for towers at Brook, Brighstone and Atherfield Point, the only defensive measure executed in the area was a military road from Chale to Freshwater. This permitted the speedy reinforcement of threatened beaches.

In the West Wight, Fort Victoria, Fort Albert and Yarmouth Castle were reduced to reserve status, but Freshwater Redoubt was retained to protect the rear of the coast batteries on the 'Freshwater Isle'. It was easier to defend the Needles Passage than Spithead. The ship channel was squeezed between shoal water and the cliffs which ran from the Needles Rocks to Cliff End, at a range of no more than 2,000 yards (1829 m). Four new clifftop batteries were built: Needles Point (six guns), Hatherwood (seven guns), Warden Point (eight guns) and Cliff End (nine guns). All guns were mounted in open emplacements because of the height of the cliffs, (seldom less than 100 feet/30.5m) but the cliffs themselves were so unstable that a great deal of money had to be spent on draining them.

Here, too, landward defences were minimal. Needles had a deep ditch, Warden Point and Cliff End brick walls and caponiers, but Hatherwood had no defences at all. To support all four a hexagonal fortified barracks was built at Golden Hill with six rooftop guns covering both the rear of the batteries and the line of the River Yar to the east.

Hurst Castle was too low-lying for the open batteries added in 1852 to withstand concentrated broadsides from ironclads. The answer was to add to the Tudor castle granite wing batteries with iron shields which eventually housed 41 guns, but at a staggering cost of £220,000.

In 1866 the British army reverted to muzzle-loading guns because weaknesses in the design of the Armstrong gun meant they were underpowered and lacked penetration. The new rifled muzzle-loaders (RMLs) retained many of Armstrong's innovations, including rifling and the strengthening of the barrel by placing successive heated tubular jackets of wrought-iron over the inner tube. These shrank into place as they cooled. The RML sat on a wrought-iron or steel garrison carriage and inclined traversing platform (or 'slide'). When the gun was fired the recoil drove the carriage up the incline until it was stopped, either by meshing together friction plates on the upper and lower carriages or by the compression of a piston within an oil-filled cylinder. After the ramming home of cartridge and shell, the gun was run down the incline for firing. The platform could be traversed on iron 'racer' tracks set into granite blocks in the emplacement floor. A 9-inch RML on a replica simplified carriage and slide can be seen today at Old Needles Battery. Shells and guns were listed either by weight (e.g. 64-pounder) or by diameter (e.g. 7-inch).

Yet the arguments for breech-loading were still powerful and the introduction of steel guns with interrupted screw breeches in 1881 presaged the end of muzzle-loading for good. New types of smokeless powder needed long barrels in which to develop their full power. Even so, attempts were made to utilize the large quantities of available RML barrels. At Puckpool in 1889 an experiment in auto-loading was made with the construction of two emplacements for a special 10.4-inch calibre RML. In the 1890s, mountings for 9-inch RML guns which permitted higher elevation and longer range were installed at Hatherwood, Warden Point and a new and short-lived battery at Steyne Wood, Bembridge.

They were all culs-de-sac. In the mid-1880s the breech-loading steel gun came of age. The traversing slide was replaced by fixed mountings in which the gun recoiled hydropneumatically in a 'cradle' on a central drum. The two most important coast defence breech-loaders (BLs) were the 9-inch and the 6-inch. The former opposed battleships, the latter cruisers and blockships, roles the same weapons retained until the termination of coast defence in 1956. New concrete barbette emplacements were built in which the guns fired over a low concrete wall.

The development in the 1880s of steam-driven torpedo-boats capable of 30 knots posed a new threat to naval anchorages which the old RMLs were too cumbersome and slow-loading to deter. The answer was the quick-firing (QF) gun which

traversed quickly and could fire up to 25 shells a minute. Metal cartridge cases were fixed to the shells, so reloading was immediate: the delay caused by washing out embers from bagged cartridges was thus avoided. After 3-pounder and 6-pounder shells proved too lightweight to stop a torpedo craft, the 12-pounder and the 4.7-inch became the standard QF guns.

Old batteries were altered and additional ones built for the new guns between 1895 and 1905. 6-inch BLs and 4.7-inch QFs were emplaced on top of the Spithead sea forts. Batteries of QF guns were added to Freshwater Redoubt, Hurst Castle and the top of Fort Albert. New 9.2-inch batteries were built at Culver and Nodes Point in the East Wight and New Needles in the West Wight. 6-inch and 9.2-inch emplacements replaced the older weapons at Puckpool in the east and Warden Point in the west.

Sometimes this meant wasted effort, because 6-inch BLs were also fitted at Cliff End, duplicating the role of Warden Point, while the waters Puckpool commanded were too enclosed for her powerful weapons to be effective. If anything, there were simply too many BL guns crowded into some batteries, and in the years before 1918 armament was often reduced.

Yet it is somewhat startling to realize that, while the barrels were occasionally changed after wear, the types of guns emplaced in the Isle of Wight largely stayed the same through both world wars. As Germany replaced France as our enemy and the threat of attack came from the east, so the Portsmouth Fortress became less important. After 1905 only one entirely new battery was built on the Island, the 6-inch at Bouldnor in 1937-38. Indeed, two of the Victorian ones, Hatherwood and Redcliff, were ruined by cliff erosion. Today, after thirty years of neglect, dereliction and demolition, a tardy effort is being made to preserve at least some of the Victorian defensive system. It is little enough and only just in time.

The Island in the Second World War
BILL CURLING

The offshore Fort Albert, originally part of the Island's Victorian defences, reactivated for use in the Second World War, and now a block of luxury flats.

The Isle of Wight, of all the islands which lie off the British Isles, was most highly involved in the Second World War. As a member of Force J, the centre of our three British naval assault forces for D-Day, my most vivid memory of it is on the eve of the invasion on June 5th, 1944, as an amateur sailor in one of a mighty armada of ships of all shapes and sizes which went out of the eastern end of the Solent past Bembridge on its north eastern corner and headed for France.

This lovely island in its long history has often been under threat of invasion since the Romans conquered it in AD 43 and left their mark at such places as Brading and Newport. The Normans subsequently conquered it and the French raided it and occupied parts of it, like Newtown. In fact, not till the defeat of the Spanish Armada 400 years ago and our eventual naval supremacy in the Channel, were the Islanders reasonably free from the threat of invasion.

If we had not won the Battle of Britain no doubt the Germans would have invaded the Island in the early 1940s. David Niven, a brilliant actor and a gallant commando soldier, captured documents from a German officer which clearly showed that the Germans intended to take the

Island. The Germans appreciated the Island's vital importance to the Royal Navy. If Portsmouth and the Solent had not been usable, no successful amphibious invasion of north west France would have been possible.

I do not expect many people to remember after half a century how the Islanders suffered in the Second World War. They did not suffer in the same way as Londoners, the people of Portsmouth, Southampton and Coventry, who were all badly blitzed, but they had more than their share of air raids and doodlebugs. The skilled Royal Observer Corps officer H.J.T. Leal, in his illuminating record of the air raids over the Island, recalls that in round figures 500 people in the Island were either killed or seriously injured and another 300 had minor injuries. Nearly 11,000 buildings were destroyed or damaged, of which the towns of Cowes and Ventnor fared worst. Ventnor with its radar station was a legitimate target. So was Cowes, for not only was J. Samuel White an important ship-building yard, but Saunders Roe, who made Walrus and Sea Otter flying boats and other weapons of war, were aiding the war effort.

I suppose many Islanders had near misses. I still remember a raid on Cowes in 1943 when my wife and I and our two eldest children sheltered under a stout dining room table in the house in Park Road where we were lodging.

The Morton twins, Cavendish and Concord, both skilled artists who were doing highly technical work in East Cowes, had their lucky escapes. Cavendish Morton, now best known of all Bembridge people with his lovely seascapes, recalls that when he was doing his daily business after breakfast, there was a very near miss on a nearby sewer. It was not a painful occasion but very, very unpleasant.

I think every Islander will remember personal experiences of buildings wrecked. Those who go down Cowes High Street and pause at the post office will see next to it the Spar grocery shop, started by the family of Hewitt in the year 1790 and until recently run by the direct descendants of the founder. The Spar is now a single-storey building. On either side of it are two two-storey buildings — one of them the post office. The reason: Hewitts before the war was likewise a two-storey building but received almost a direct hit from a land-mine which killed a man, demolished the building and badly damaged the war memorial nearby.

At our cottage on The Point, Bembridge, over-looking the Solent and in the First World War, part of the officers' mess of the seaplane base on Bembridge Point, we survived unscathed but along the beach to the east the Garland Club, which had been a feature of Bembridge in pre-war days, was destroyed.

Cowes had its worst moments of the war in 1942 when in the first week of May enemy aircraft attacked in strength. Fortunately the Polish destroyer *Blyskawica* was at J. Samuel White's yard for a refit. She had had a near miss in an earlier raid at the end of April. Her gun crews fought like demons to save their ship and the citizens of Cowes on that May night — their courage being commemorated for all time on a plaque near Osborne Court.

I did not join Force J till towards the end of 1942. Our headquarters in Cowes were in what is now Osborne Court. The senior officers in the Force lived in the Royal Yacht Squadron premises nearby. Others were, I think, in the Gloucester Hotel. Married officers were allowed to find lodgings in the town until D-Day approached.

Almost my first job on joining Force J was to be in charge of Gurnard Pines Camp. In the attractive Victorian building were housed a mix-ture of naval and army officers, and in the Nissen huts in the grounds nearby were the communi-cations ratings, signalmen and telegraphists. The army officers outnumbered the sailors in the big house. They were gunners — bombardment liaison officers (B.L.O.s) or forward observation officers (F.O.O.s). The idea was that in the invasion the army in the early stages would need support from the big guns of ships at sea. The F.O.O.s would be with each unit of advancing troops. An F.O.O. (supported by a naval tele-graphist with a portable wireless set) would ask by wireless for a naval bombardment on certain German strong points from his opposite number, the B.L.O. in one of the bombarding ships. Good communications between B.L.O. and F.O.O. might be vital, so plenty of exercises had to be taken in the Island before D-Day.

I think there were about 200 communications ratings in Gurnard Camp. Most of them were for beach signal units. On landing each naval beach master needed his own beach signal unit which landed early on D-Day. We expected them to have heavy casualties as had happened at Salerno in Italy but they were destined to be fairly lucky in Force J. The beach master I particularly remember was bearded Captain Colin Maud, a much-decorated destroyer captain, known to his friends as Whiskers, who loved the Island and spent the last years of his life in Bembridge.

Commanding Force J when I joined was Captain C.J. Hughes-Hallett, whom we usually referred to behind his back as Hughes-Hitler. He was said by his contemporaries to be bossy, but he ended his naval career as Vice-Admiral Sir Charles Hughes-Hallett; so he was clearly a very distinguished sailor.

My immediate boss in Force J as signal officer was Lieutenant Peter Howes, a very dashing signal officer, who later became an admiral and near the end of his working days right hand man to the Lord Mayor of London.

The Pines Camp is now a large well-run holiday village: a mixture of caravans and chalets with a large swimming pool and many attractions. The only sad thing is that the big house has been razed to the ground. Gurnard has grown greatly since I knew it in the war, but from the Pines there is still the same view across the Solent and below is the marshy ground and the little stream, the Luck, which flows into Gurnard Bay.

I had not long been at Gurnard before Force J began to expand greatly in size and two other assault forces of similar size were formed: Force S and Force G. General Montgomery, as he then was, and other leaders realized that if the amphibious invasion of Europe was to succeed we had to think big.

In the end, not only were there three British assaulting divisions but two American and, on our left, the 6th Airborne Division, who were to play a vital role protecting our left flank and securing important bridges and roads near Caen, supported by Royal Marine Commandos and other commandos, a good proportion of whom did much of their training in the Isle of Wight.

I had not been at Gurnard long when 'Hughes-Hitler' was succeeded by a more senior officer, the future Admiral Sir Philip Vian, of Cossack fame. He was one of the most brilliant destroyer captains of the war, an outstanding fighting sailor with big dark bushy eyebrows, who did not suffer fools gladly.

Before Admiral Vian arrived at Cowes I had left Gurnard to act temporarily as signal officer to GJ3 under Captain A.F. Pugsley. His headquarters were at Lepe House at the entrance to Beaulieu River on the other side of the Solent from Gurnard and, as the crow flies, only about four miles NNW of Gurnard Bay.

Under Pugsley we carried out a full-scale exercise carrying men of one of the Canadian brigades in merchant ships right down the East Solent and along the south coast heading east to Brighton. We then turned south towards France, no doubt hoping the Germans would learn of our exercise and expect us to assault in the future near Calais.

The exercise I remember best in the Island was on Arreton Down half a mile east of the thatched-roofed Hare and Hounds Inn on the chalk down to the south of the road running from the Hare and Hounds towards Brading. It was good country for practising naval communications, with a lovely view to the west and Arreton village below – a down on which King Charles I had once met Sir John Oglander of Nunwell, a member of one of the oldest and most distinguished of Island families.

Arreton has always had a special place in my heart since that exercise nearly fifty years ago; Arreton's church of great age, Arreton Manor and Arreton Vicarage, with its attractive garden, all hiding below one in the valley. What is more, it is amazing to think that, according to Druidical tradition, the stones of Stonehenge were brought over from France via Brading Haven and hauled up to the summit of Arreton Down, where they were first erected before being moved later to Salisbury Plain.

Of course preparations and practices for D-Day were going on in various parts of the Island and along the Dorset, Hampshire and Sussex coasts north of the Island.

From the beginning of the war there had been coastal batteries on such places as Culver Down in East Wight, with 9.2 inch guns guarding the eastern entrance to the Solent, and at the Needles, guarding the western entrance. The forts protecting Spithead were all manned – St Helen's Fort, with Bembridge point due south of it, and Node's Point due west; No Man's Land Fort, NNW of the now-vanished Seaview pier; Horse Sand Fort, NW of No Man's Land Fort; and Spitbank Fort near the entrance to Portsmouth Harbour. They were all connected by cable and played an important rôle in the anti-submarine defences of Portsmouth.

The Royal Marines, including their Special Service commandos, were much involved in training on the Island before D-Day. David Niven and Brian Franks, two of the founder members of the Bembridge Sailing Dinghy Club in pre-war days, were in the same commando under Lord Lovat, and trained near Wootton Creek. The story goes that Niven had a great affair with a Wootton girl but D-Day came just too soon! His mother lived at Rose Cottage, in Bembridge, High Strret, where the Flory family now live. David was so full of 'go' that his mother decided to build a self-contained suite at the back of the house against the garden wall for the use of David and his friends. It was known as David's Sin-Bin.

Next to Rose Cottage is Willow Cottage, where the Sloley Family now live. Bill Sloley was a Royal Marine. One of the Royal Marine Commandos, No 40, went from Cowes with Force J to Dieppe, and afterwards returned to the Shanklin and Ventnor area to be housed in civilian billets as, in 1942, were No 41 Royal Marine Commando in Ryde, Seaview, St Helens and Bembridge, the officers being billeted in Bembridge House, then owned by General Sir Michael West. One of the unit, Jan Maley, married a Bembridge girl and is now a respected parish councillor.

No 41 left the Island at the end of 1942, took part in the invasion of Sicily, and two months later had a very bad time at Salerno, landing with some 200 casualties. Bill Sloley was one of those who joined this commando after Salerno.

No 2 Battalion Royal Marines was based at Ryde in 1942, the officers being billeted in Ryde's Royal Esplanade Hotel. Beti's coffee house was a favourite meeting place when off duty in the day-time, the Starboard Club in Seaview in the evenings. Bill Sloley still remembers, 45 years on, that morale was much improved for many by the appearances in Ryde Town Hall of Phyllis Dixey as the Peek-a-boo Girl. She was definitely good for the war effort.

No 46 Royal Marine Commando was billeted at Upper Chine School before D-Day, doing many of their exercises in that part of East Wight, not far from Ventnor Radar Station, whose Wrens played an important rôle.

As the spring of 1944 came in everyone realized that D-Day was approaching. I still vividly remember General Montgomery and the outstanding South African leader, General Smuts, with his distinctive three-cornered hat, coming down to Cowes to address the 3rd Canadian Division team and the Force J team. Both were eloquent speakers and the Canadians, who had suffered so severely at Dieppe, were much heartened, as were the British.

Our superiority in the air was now pronounced, helped by growing American air strength. Although German aircraft continued to attack Island targets early in 1944, they were on a small scale compared with the attack on Cowes in May 1942, and no great damage was done. It was essential that we should control the air as D-Day approached.

Everyone was naturally apprehensive. Most of the Force J team went to a special service in Holy Trinity Church, Cowes, before we were due to depart. Standing at the back of the Squadron building, the church had been consecrated in 1832 "as the church in Cowes foreshore for sailors and seafarers" and is full of memorials to famous yachtsmen. Three of those remembered are Sir Hercules Langrishe, one of the all-time greats amongst yachtsmen, who died in 1943 after being a member of the Squadron for over 50 years; Sir Philip Hunloke, sailing master to King George VI and in charge of *Britannia* to the end of his racing days; and Sir Ralph Gore, who lived at The Watch House, Bembridge, Commodore of the Squadron and another highly skilled helmsman. It was perhaps right that we should assemble in "the seafarers church" and pray that things would go well for us all in the days ahead.

As I have said, I shall never forget the armada of ships which sailed out of the east end of the Solent on 6th June, 1944. In vivid contrast to the Norwegian campaign of 1940, when our ships were frequently bombed, we now had control of the air, which gave the greatest amphibious operation in history a chance of success. As everyone now knows, we were successful as a result of good planning and the great courage shown by so many from all over the British Empire; from our allies from America, from the Free French and from all who hated Naziism.

The Isle of Wight Hunt
MICHAEL POLAND

The Isle of Wight Hunt is unique. As the oldest established sporting organization on the Island, it is also the only island foxhunt in the world. Furthermore, it was directly responsible for both the fox and the badger being introduced to the Island. To cap it all, during Queen Victoria's reign, it had a close association with Royalty which was the envy of the country.

So close, indeed, was the Hunt's relationship with the Royal Family that in 1845, when the Crockford Harriers were replaced by the foxhounds, the entire pack was bought by the Prince of Wales and kennelled at Windsor. The Prince himself once hunted with the hounds from Rowborough, and Princess Beatrice (the Queen's daughter), Prince Henry of Battenberg (the Queen's son-in-law) and the Empress of Austria were regular followers of the Hunt.

Queen Victoria, who used to enjoy seeing the hounds hunting around Osborne House, twice paid the Hunt a special compliment. Firstly, during her state drive from Osborne to Newport as part of her Golden Jubilee celebrations, the 24 outriders were all from the Hunt, the 12 preceding the royal carriage wearing scarlet, and the 12 following in black hunt coats. Secondly, in 1888, she engaged the then Huntsman, John Harvey Jnr, as Huntsman to the Queen's Buckhounds at Windsor.

The fox was not indigenous to the Island, and apart from some exclusive deer hunting around Appuldurcombe, hare hunting with harriers proved the popular sport. An episode in 1830, however, caused all this to change.

Parson Fenwick's pet fox was the sole one on the Island. One day it escaped from its kennel at Brook, could not be caught and started to cause havoc as it regularly raided chicken houses and lambing areas. In response to widespread pleas from farmers, Squire Thatcher, who was Master of the Crockford Harriers and kept·them at his home, Wacklands, agreed to see how he could help, but was mindful that his hounds were trained to hunt only hare.

During the Christmas week of 1830, however, conditions were right and the fox was viewed away by farmers cutting gorse on Brook Down. A fine hunt followed before, to the relief of the farmers, the fox was caught. Interestingly, it ran by coverts and farms which still exist today, and are often the scene of present-day hunts. Running by Pitt Place, to Barnes High where he was turned, to Troopers, he went on to Presford Farm, before swinging right to Kingston Copse and then making for the Wilderness. Then, climbing Ramsdown, the fox ran Chillerton Downs, skirting Westridge, before going through Lorden's, down to Haslet Farm, across to Buck's Farm, and then making to Dungewood where hounds caught him. Fifteen miles as hounds ran, with a furthest point of $6^3/_4$ miles. By any standards, this was a truly remarkable hunt, especially as it was the first time the hounds had hunted a fox. One can only assume that the hounds then were much slower than foxhounds are today.

To celebrate the great and successful occasion, that evening Farmer Day of Westcourt held a party which, by all accounts, was up to the Island's best standards. Wine and punch flowed freely, Squire Thatcher became much the worse for wear, repeatedly mumbling as he was helped to a couch – "I killed the fox. I killed the fox" – thus gaining the name of the 'Fox Slayer'. When the party broke up at 3.00 am, there was total chaos, the revellers first being unable to identify their own horses, and then undecided on which side they should mount!

Great Island families, such as the Bartons, Cottons, Nunns, Harveys, Jolliffes, Mews and Youngs, whose successors are with us today, were amongst the most prominent revellers. In a contentious speech, after proposing the toast to the Queen and Hunting, Day proposed there should be a pack of foxhounds on the Island. Such had been the excitement of the day's hunt, there was no lack of agreement. Only Squire Thatcher, despite his pride at his hounds' success, was adamant that the fox did not present a worthy substitute for the hare, and dug his heels in. Hence, the hare continued as the quarry.

Memories of the eventful day, however, refused to depart and it was the Squire's son, Will, who eventually engineered the change.

Before the meet ... the Master and the hounds in 1990.

the fox population began to thrive to the extent that now the whole Island can be termed 'well foxed'.

The Squire, still ignorant of the latest arrivals, arranged to hold the traditional Opening Meet for his harriers in his Wacklands grounds. As luck would have it, the harriers took a line into the withybed where they put up a fox, and via Hale, Budbridge, Godshill and Bleak Down, ran to the Wilderness where they lost him. At first, the Master was puzzled by the unusual line for a hare before the truth dawned upon him. A hare hunter to the last, his vile temper knew no bounds, swearing that if he could find the rascal who had introduced the foxes, he would lay his hunting whip across his shoulders!

Importing the foxes as they did would, rightly, not be countenanced today and the severest penalties would follow, but the event must be judged against the totally different standards of the time.

Two years later, Mr Benjamin Cotton of Afton Manor, Freshwater, had the courage to found the Island's first, and only, pack of foxhounds. Whether it was coincidence, or whether Squire Thatcher had failed to recover from his outburst, he died in 1845, the same year as the foxhounds were started, and his beloved harriers were sold to the Prince of Wales.

The fox is now a popular part of the Island's culture, and the Hunt may also take full credit for importing the badger. Previously, it simply did not exist on the Island, but in the 1920s, Mr John Willis Fleming, then Master, became alarmed as an outbreak of mange endangered the whole fox population. Taking advice from friends on the mainland, he imported a dozen badgers (whose crates still exist today) and turned them out. His plan was a complete success, for the badgers drove the foxes away from their diseased earths and cleaned them, and the foxes were forced to open fresh earths.

Today, the Island enjoys a popular and healthy badger population, and it is particularly noteworthy that they thrived and prospered without receiving any special favours from the Hunt.

Sadly, the Hunt suffered a succession of short Masterships and until General Sir Henry Daly took over in 1881, there had been no fewer than twelve different Masters. Successful hunts depend upon the continuity provided by stable Masterships, and with hindsight, it is a great

Bitten by the foxhunting bug on his visits to the mainland, Will became increasingly frustrated at his father's obstinacy until, in 1843, he learnt that a dealer in Portsmouth had eight foxes for sale.

The whole operation was furtively carried out and in the greatest secrecy. Will put them into four hampers and brought them over on the ferry to Ryde where their smell survived inquisitive enquiry before he finally reached the safety of Newchurch. To be found out would have incurred the wrath of both his father and the farmers. Finally, that evening when the Squire was satisfied with his dinner and snoring in his armchair, Will and his accomplice crept away and turned out the foxes, some in the withybed behind the house, and the others in a nearby wood.

History does not relate whether Will was alone in his mainland sorties, but from that time shame that the Hunt's early days must have been blighted by instability. The Island had great potential to be a really successful Hunt and, if it had been properly exploited, it would have left us today with really outstanding sport and riding – amongst the best in the country.

General Daly's Mastership lasted from 1881 to 1889, the longest up to then. His main claim to distinction, however, lay off the hunting field. He is the only British officer ever to go into action wearing a velvet hunting cap. At the storming of Delhi, when a young subaltern, he was granted permission to don the hunting cap to protect him from the missiles being thrown down by the mutineers. Indeed, this incident may have been the forerunner of the military helmet. He was followed as Master shortly afterwards in 1894 by the Irish Colonel Howard Brooke, whose reign lasted until 1916 and still is the longest on record.

The Willis Flemings, who have had such a beneficial influence on the Hunt, were first involved in the Mastership in 1920. Mr John Willis Fleming, he who introduced the badgers, was Master until 1925 and his son, the indomitable Brigadier, was later Master from 1966 to 1968.

Several famous foxhunters have held the Isle of Wight Mastership. Colonel C M Wellesley-Wesley's term of office, 1933-1935, was unusual in as much as at the same time he was also the successful Master of the South Dorset Hunt.

That most distinguished foxhunter, Mr Arthur Dalgety, was Master and Huntsman from 1955-1959. Although only a short period, the memories of it have lasted much longer! A natural countryman and a brilliant houndman, he was of a slightly volatile nature which tended to undo much of the undoubted good he did for the Hunt. He brought with him his famous white hounds and pack of beagles, all of which were kennelled at Gatcombe where, at one time, over 100 couple of hounds were kennelled. The white hounds were his particular pride and joy, but there was trouble with sheep, so he had them all put down. Nevertheless, he so opened up the country and so enthused many young and keen foxhounters that today, 30 years later, his influence is still strong.

Mr John Dix succeeded in 1959, and remained until 1965. Bringing his own hounds from the Dartmoor, he looked after the pack himself, often employing female assistance. One girl, Rachel Green, went on to become the country's first female professional Huntsman. Attracted by the freedom of having his own private pack with neither committee nor subscribers, John Dix is now Master of his own pack in Cardiganshire, the Llangeitho. In 1987 he had to retire from hunting hounds, and his professional Huntsman is Miss Mandy Pritchard, from Ryde.

Mr John Kingswell, on his own or with Joints from 1962 to 1983, was another Master of note. A farmer from one of the Island's oldest families, he became a popular Master and left a first class pack of hounds to the present régime. The modern Isle of Wight Hunt owes much to his hard work and influence.

No Mastership is complete without a good hunt servant – the professional who day in and day out looks after the hounds and brings them to their peak of fitness. Sometimes, he actually hunts the hounds; he might be Kennel-Huntsman, assisting an amateur Huntsman, or a Whipper-in, helping to control the hounds. Today, the most talked-about is Harry Kennett, who was Huntsman from 1940 to 1955. His children and grandchildren, most of whom live on the Island, have all inherited a strong love for the chase, and wherever hounds are hunting here, you will usually find a Kennett. Son Teddy was, until recently, Huntsman to the Isle of Wight Foot Beagles, and another son is Kennel-Huntsman to the Milvain (Percy) in Northumberland.

A legend in his own lifetime is Bill Marks, Huntsman or Kennel-Huntsman from 1965 until his retirement in 1983. He is still living on the Island and stories of him are legion, usually concerning daring equestrian feats. The Hunt staff are employed by the Masters and, de-pending upon finances, there are usually two or three within the Isle of Wight Kennels. When times were lean, however, and for some years they were, Bill Marks coped single-handed.

Nigel Cox was Kennel-Huntsman from 1983 to 1985, and is now the successful Huntsman to the Albrighton Hounds near Wolverhampton. The present incumbent is Stephen Clifton, who came to the Island in 1985.

Each Mastership makes its own impact on the hounds. Arthur Dalgety was an expert houndman, but his impact receded when John Dix brought his own hounds with him. He, too, was a successful hound breeder and won the South of England Bitch Championship with Linnett in 1963. On his departure with most of the hounds, John Kingswell had to re-build the pack, relying heavily upon the Brocklesby (the family pack of the Earl of Yarborough, who has strong Island connections) and the Garth and South Berks. In recent years, the most sought after of the modern lines have been introduced, including the Beaufort, Exmoor, and the New Forest Welsh outcross.

A good hound needs to be fast, and to possess a good nose, cry, and stamina. He is therefore of a very athletic build, capable of galloping freely all day, and of coping with steep hills, sheepwire fences and thick undergrowth and woodlands. The Isle of Wight hound (of which there are 24 couple in kennel) can do all this, and a particular feature is his marvellous cry.

Because of our geographical position, it is unlikely our best doghounds will ever be in demand for stud purposes, but the pack is more than making its mark with its reputation. Hounds are bred to hunt, and showing is merely a bonus, but in 1988, the pack had its most successful show season ever, winning coveted prizes at the main hound shows at Peterborough, Honiton and Ardingly. At Ardingly, it entered ten classes and won seven first prizes, including the doghound reserve championship.

The kennels are at Gatcombe in purpose-built premises owned by a syndicate formed in 1927. In the early days, the kennel location depended largely upon where the Master lived, and hence Afton, Marvel, Appuldurcombe and Wootton have all at one time been home to the hounds. Gatcombe, however, is ideal. Situated in the middle of the Island, it is a perfect centre from which to walk out or exercise hounds. They now form an integral part of the village culture, as the hounds overlook most of the houses, and their melodious singing in kennel can be heard up to three miles away.

The Hunt is mostly financed by sub-scription, day caps, donations and Hunt functions, including those run by the independent Ladies, Point-to-Point and Supporters' Club Committees. The balance has to be found by the Masters. Throughout the year, some 4,000-5,000 people support the Hunt in one form or another, making it an integral part of the Island's social fabric. Indeed, with the exception of the Cowes Week Balls held for the benefit of visitors, the Hunt Ball must rank as the top social function.

Without the farming community, however, the Hunt simply could not exist. Hunting enjoys no divine right – it depends entirely upon the invitation or agreement of farmers and in this respect the Hunt is indeed lucky. It enjoys enormous goodwill and support from the farming community and the shooting fraternity. Although some might only have a slight exposure to the Hunt, the majority of the Island's farmers are fiercely proud and jealous of the Hunt. In return, the Hunt is ever grateful to them.

Since Parson Fenwick's fox was hunted nearly 160 years ago, the Hunt has come a long way and seen many milestones. It is justly proud of its reputation and achievements, and as long as it continues to receive such encouragement from the Island people, it will continue to thrive.

The Isle Of Wight Foot Beagles
PHILIP MITCHESON

A pack of beagles was first raised in the Island by Henry Young of East Standen Manor, near Newport, in 1906. Although there have been inevitable breaks occasioned by two world wars, when hunting had to be suspended and the packs dispersed, beagling on the Island has continued from that date.

For a period between 1923 and 1940, and indeed prior even to the outbreak of the First World War in 1914, Francis Mew (later Lieutenant Colonel) and his sister, members of a well-known Newport family, had also hunted a pack of their own. Then in 1949 Arthur Dalgety, on becoming Master of the Isle of Wight Foxhounds, brought his own small beagle pack across the Solent and hunted them from time to time, until he left the Island in 1960. The previous year a meeting had been held at Kingston Manor, Mew's house near Chale, called by the owner and Denys Danby to test the probable measure of public support; and as a result the beagle pack as we know it today was reformed with drafts obtained from a number of mainland packs. The new pack began hunting in the following autumn and there are, it is nice to report, still a number of those early followers in the field at the present time.

It is only right, I think, to place on record the debt owed to Mew and his family for their long and generous support, and also to Denys Danby who, a veterinary surgeon by profession, was very valuable to the pack, as well as being one of the finest amateur beagle huntsmen of his day. Sadly, neither of them is now with us. Mew was Master or Joint Master from the re-formation of the pack in 1959 until his death in December 1984. He was joined by Denys Danby until his death in 1968, and then by Major General Sir Robert Pigot, Bart (1968-82). After Mew's death the present writer became Master from 1985 until 1987. I was joined in 1986 by today's Master, Dr M.L.R. Davies.

For a time the newly established pack was kennelled with the Foxhounds at Staplers and, as the Honorary Secretary, I was required to walk them out three times a week 'for a good hour' at 7 a.m. before lessons began at Little Appley, a prep school in Ryde owned and run by my

Beagling in the rain ... Lieutenant-Colonel Mitcheson discusses the day's prospects with kennelman Brodie at the White Lion, Arreton.

brother and me. Colonel Mew decided that the pack should be bred small in size - 13 to 14½ inches at the shoulder, as compared with a more usual 15 to 16 inches. This relatively small size of hound is inevitably reflected in the number of hares accounted for each season - normally five or six brace (a tally often considerably exceeded by packs of larger hounds on the mainland). But set against this there is the undoubted advantage that followers are enabled to see more hound-work than when out with a pack of larger hounds. This surely is to the advantage of all who hunt, or follow, hounds.

Some ten years or more ago, Colonel Mew decided, on the basis of long and exceptional experience in hound-breeding, that, probably for one litter only, he would see what, if any, advantage was to be gained from the putting of a beagle dog-hound to a rough-coated French basset bitch of hunting stock, which he duly acquired after a fairly lengthy correspondence. This, when read by me much later, proved quite amusing, as neither party to the arrangement had much of the other's language.

In due course a mixed litter of eight puppies was produced which, for the lack of a better name, and because all were markedly rough-coated, were referred to as 'Fluffies', and caused considerable interest both in kennels and in the hunting field. When they were duly entered to hunting some two years later, the results proved quite interesting to followers. On the credit side was the fact that, being considerably larger and heavier hounds, they slowed the pack down quite considerably and steadied them, which in itself was not a bad thing. They hunted with a deep and lovely cry which was easily recognizable. But on the debit side, no doubt because of their larger size and weight, they proved 'terrible fighters' in kennel, and soon had to be lodged separately - with their numbers, as well as that of our own beagles, somewhat reduced by then. The last of them - a bitch called Nina - had finally to be put down at a considerable age and well after her hunting days were over, during my brief period of Mastership. It proved an interesting, and by no means unrewarding experience, but it was not repeated.

After hunting with the pack for some 30 years there are many memories to fall back on, but two or three only must suffice.

On one occasion a few years ago now, on the downland above Dean Farm at Whitwell - a favourite place for cliff walkers and their dogs, after a first-rate hunt the hounds were about to earn their just reward when a labrador, being walked by a woman of nearby Niton village, intervened to course the hare, immediately ahead of the pack, and in the resulting confusion they went unrewarded. As Honorary Secretary and, in those days, Hunting Correspondent to the *County Press* and other papers, I was instructed by Francis Mew to include a mention of this unwarranted intrusion "by a local cur dog". As was to be expected, this quickly resulted in a furious letter to the paper by the owner, pointing out to the public at large that her dog was of impeccable pedigree. I was instructed by Francis

to reply, and did, to the effect that dogs were held to be of two kinds only – hounds and curs – and no other. The owner was not pleased to be so advised.

On another occasion, when hunting from The Woodman's Arms at Wootton Common, I was, as a Whipper-in, on Briddlesford farmland, watching over a run of hedge leading up towards the farmhouse. Denys Danby was hunting hounds, which came away from a narrow strip of nearby woodland in full cry, but on the wrong quarry - a farmyard cat. Quite correctly I called out "Wor (beware) cat", to warn the Huntsman. Whereupon there was a roar from Francis Mew, with whom he was Joint-Master and of whom I had not been aware on the far side of the thick hedge, "Why did you tell him, you b....y fool", and relations were a little strained for a few days – but soon restored.

I remember, too, as I am sure he will still, that on the same day Harry Kennett, whipping-in, was almost drowned falling awkwardly into a deep pool of water in the same stretch of wood.

And on yet another occasion I was standing with Francis on Signal Hill, at Porchfield, when a hard-hunted hare 'clapt' within feet of us and a bitch hound, name long forgotten, on a screaming scent, came to a brief check with her front feet on the hare's back. This was too much. She leapt up, threw the hound backwards head over heels and, as I seem to remember, made good her escape after a further hunt ... But enough of memories.

In conclusion, I should not want to end this brief account of so many happy days spent beagling in the Island without expressing the gratitude of many to Teddy Kennett, who has hunted hounds so well since Denys Danby was compelled to give up, sadly through ill-health; and to Harry Kennett, who has turned hounds to him for some thirty years (both of them widely known throughout the Island); also to the Brodies, husband and wife, who have cared for hounds in kennels for the same long period.

Floreat venatio

Yacht Clubs and
Yachting in the Isle of Wight
HARRY CHILLINGWORTH

Sailing for pleasure or for commercial reasons around the shores of the Isle of Wight has taken place for many hundreds of years. It is, however, only in the first half of the 19th century that the earliest mention of competitive racing and the formation of yacht clubs occurs.

Commercial sailing in the past must include the well-known Island pastime of smuggling. Traffic in contraband goods was extensively carried on between the Island and the coast of France. The 'Back of the Wight' was a 'no-go area' for outsiders and, indeed, 'the law' generally allowed those Islanders engaged in smuggling to carry on much as they wished. But all these activities died out during the last century and sailing took on a more recreational character.

It was during the early part of the 19th century that the first Isle of Wight yacht club was established, when in 1815 the Royal Yacht Squadron opened its doors to an exclusive membership; the same year as Napoleon Bonaparte was defeated and Wellington immortalized. The first meeting of this club actually took place at the Thatched House Tavern in St James's Street, London, with Lord Grantham (later, Earl de Grey) in the chair; it was simply styled 'The Yacht Club'. In all 42 members were present at this first meeting. Many of the names of those present have to this day retained strong Isle of Wight connections. The first elected commodore was the Earl of Yarborough, to whom an obelisk stands on the top of Culver Down. The Royal Yacht Squadron acquired its present name in 1833 when His Majesty William IV "graciously approved an institution of such national utility". We read that the conditions and privileges of membership were: 1) Any gentleman being a bona fide owner of a British yacht of 30 tons or more was eligible for admission, 2) The subscription was an annual payment of £8, with an entrance fee of £15, 3) Honorary Members paid no subscription, except that those who used the house and reading room paid £1 annually, 4) Each yacht was authorized by the Lords of the Admiralty to wear St George's Ensign and was admitted into all foreign ports, free of dues, being similar in this respect to men-of-war.

In the early days of yacht racing the contests were referred to as Matches and were mostly sailed from Cowes Roads, either round the Wight or, maybe, on a course round the Nab Light and back round a buoy off Yarmouth. All the yachts taking part were large cutters with gaff rigs, owned by wealthy men and handled by a professional crew. The Matches were fought out for a substantial wager or, sometimes, a wager and a cup. Many of the Matches were more in the nature of a naval engagement than a race. Several of the yachts of this era had cannon and side-arms on board - just in case. Discipline on board was strict and definitely service style. It is said that the Earl of Yarborough, although much loved by all who came in contact with him, would not hesitate to have an offending crewman flogged.

It is not surprising that we find many reports of heated engagements between contending yachts in which blows would be exchanged. Sir James Jordan is reported as having had a narrow escape from a dreadful blow aimed at the back of his head with a handspike, by one of Mr Weld's men, when their two yachts, *Arrow* and *Miranda*, became entangled in a race. Sir James avoided the blow and "hitting out left and right, floored the rascal with tremendous violence"! There is no need to add that the Royal Yachting Association and Rules of Racing had to wait a further 30 years before coming into being.

An essential of all large yachts was a good crew and one job that the secretary of the Royal Yacht Squadron had, in those early days, was that of keeping a blacklist of undesirable hands who might have misbehaved, ashore or afloat, in the past. The yacht was controlled by a Master who held the title as the paid hand in charge of the vessel, and it is the same title which today we give to the captain of a merchant ship who holds a Master's certificate. The title of Captain is only applied to the commanding officer of a ship of the Royal Navy.

It was William Cooper who advised, in his treatise *The Yacht Sailor*, published in the mid-19th century, that "an elderly, steady and strictly sober man" would be suitable for the job of Master of a yacht. He went on to recommend that the sailing rig for Masters "should be fine blue cloth and a rough suit for wet weather, dress cap and oilskin hat without a band" – outward appearance in those days was all important. He said that the men's clothing should be: "pilot cloth pea jackets, trousers of the same material and blue woollen shirts, made man-of-war fashion with rolling collars, loose bodies and sleeves gathered into pleats at the wrists, neat oilskin covered hats showing straw on the underneath part of the leaf; the light reflected from the straw gives the man's face a bright cheerful expression".

After 1833, when the Royal Yacht Squadron received its present name, quite a few yacht clubs were formed under royal patronage. The Royal London had its first meeting in 1838, followed by the Royal Victoria in 1845 and the Royal Southern in 1878. It is interesting to note that many of the large houses on St John's Hill, going down into Ryde from Sandown, were built by the rich and famous, so that they could sail their yachts from the Royal Victoria club, whose building still stands near the Ryde Esplanade railway station, although the club now has moved to Wootton Creek. If we look carefully at these houses on St John's Hill, we see that nearly all have glass domes on the top of the roofs; they are believed to be where the wives could sit and watch their menfolk disporting themselves on the Solent.

During the latter half of Queen Victoria's reign yachting and small boat sailing spread widely among all the social classes and were no longer the prerogative of the wealthy. In 1886 Bembridge Sailing Club was founded, followed three years later by the Island Sailing Club and shortly afterwards by Seaview Yacht Club. All these clubs greatly widened the appeal of sailing, both as a sport and as a recreation. In addition more and more people came to live or have holidays in and around the sailing centres. It is doubtful if, at this time, there was anywhere in the world with such a concentration of sailing clubs.

At the turn of the century there was a rapid expansion of the auxiliary services which went to support the sport of sailing. In addition yacht designers came into their own and nowhere was this more evident than at Bembridge. Alf Westmacott designed the X Class and the Sunbeams which were built on the Duver at St Helens. In 1903 E.C.C. Cockburn, who lived at St Helens, won a competition for a design for a Bembridge Sailing Club One Design. This design was approved later that year by a BSC committee of three, consisting of Charlie Ricardo, Alf Westmacott and the designer himself. The Redwing Class was designed by Charles Nicholson and although not strictly a One Design class - their hulls are uniform but their rig has no

The Royal Yacht Squadron as seen from the Solent.   *(Patrick Eden/Island Life)*

Bembridge Sailing Club ... home of the Redwings.   *(Annabel Fairfax)*

restriction other than the total area of sail - it is the oldest class racing in the Solent. In more modern times the Seaview Dinghy Class was formed in 1930 and today it has 118 dinghies sailing from the club. The Solent scows are an adaptation of the much older Lymington dinghies and were first introduced at Bembridge, most of them being built at Alan Coombes's yard.

No mention of yacht designers on the Isle of Wight would be complete unless it included Uffa Fox. His career in this field began when he was only fifteen years old: "My father gave me a fine oak tree growing 75 yards from the house, on condition that I grubbed it up by the roots and so I drew up plans of a 20 ft. waterline centre board cruiser to suit this tree"; and a long life of boat design was to follow. Based in Cowes, he designed and sailed many famous yachts and class boats. He combined his design abilities with a real love of sailing.

Uffa was to recall how on one occasion, as a youngster, he attended a dance in Gurnard and after midnight set sail in his little 16 ft canoe which he had recently built. He had a good reach down the Solent and past the Needles, having a good breakfast in Swanage Bay. He then returned to Cowes by sailing back round the south side of the Island, passing through the notorious St Catherine's race with some trepidation, but without mishap, deciding to take a rest at Puckaster Cove, where he spent the night. The following day he headed out into a rough sea through Sandown Bay. The going was heavy but his little craft weathered the Bembridge Ledge buoy, whence it was a free run home to Cowes.

It would be difficult to mention all the designs for which Uffa was famous, but probably he will be best remembered for his 14 ft international dinghies, Flying Fifteens and, of course, the airborne lifeboats which he designed especially for the 1939-1945 war. In 1957 Medina Yard in Cowes built an interesting sloop, again designed by him, which was a large version of his Flying Fifteen; it was the 10.72 ton *Flying Fox* which became based in Dublin and was a very speedy craft for its day.

Of all the yachting spectacles which delight the yacht-racing connoisseur and the landlubber alike, the Island Sailing Club's Round the Island Race, held annually in June from 1931, must rank as the top event. Today it starts from the Royal Yacht Squadron line, when anything from five hundred to a thousand yachts compete. The race is now sailed westabout round the Needles, leaving Bembridge Ledge buoy to port and finishing across the Squadron line. The start is by classes, the slower yachts starting first, and this usually gives the spectator on land the chance of an unrivalled view of hundreds of yachts, usually with spinnakers set in a prevailing south-westerly wind, as they run up the Channel coast of the Island. It is the one race in the yachting calendar which enables the 'week-end sailors' to compete in friendly rivalry with the more illustrious 'professionals'; but for the majority it is sufficient to take part in this famous race, with such an armada of yachts, and the more serious matter of racing takes second place to the splendid day out on the water and a free tankard for finishing the course.

Once every two years Cowes plays host to the Admiral's Cup yachts. This international event was started in 1957 when five members of the Royal Ocean Racing Club provided a challenge cup to be competed for by national teams which were taking part in the Cowes Week regattas. The races were to include a 225-mile Channel Race and the longer 605-mile Fastnet Race. In 1957 there were only four national teams but the number has now risen to nineteen nations. In the early days it was an amateur effort, whereas today it is truly professional with highly developed and specially designed racing machines.

Several of the yacht clubs on the Island have invited the Forces sailing clubs to compete in their clubs' One Design boats. Seaview Yacht Club has, for many years, been the venue for services racing. In latter years Bembridge Sailing Club has invited the service cadets to race for a challenge cup. The Club also has long-standing competitions which are open to Public Schools, both present and past pupils.

Yacht clubs have proliferated during the past 40 years on the Isle of Wight, and many active clubs provide racing, mainly for small boat owners; Brading Haven, Yaverland, Shanklin, Yarmouth, East Cowes and Gurnard all have lively clubs, several of which have frostbite racing during the winter and also provide a wide social programme. All in all, this adds up to the Island providing a magnificent centre for design, construction and maintenance of yachts, to say nothing of the social life which goes hand in hand with this.

Royal Corinthian YC.
ROBIN COLVILLE

Cowes has many watering holes
Where sailors take their fill,
But the Royal Corinthian Yacht Club
Will always fit the bill.
Welcome's written on the mat
To those without a base
So people wander in and out
And watch the Cowes Rat Race.
Originally called Castle Rock
And owned by Rosa Lewis;
She bought it in between the wars
Thus causing quite a rumpus.
Commanding such a lovely view
Across the Solent waters
Rosa entertained in style
And made it her headquarters.
But nothing lasts forever
And after World War Two
She sold it to a syndicate
And this Club thus ensued.
It has a friendly atmosphere
Unequalled in these parts;
So come and join me for a drink
And watch the Daring Starts.

Footnote: This poem was written in 1987, before the Royal Corinthian Yacht Club was purchased by Ancasta

In Pursuit of Natural History
OLIVER H. FRAZER

The Island is almost the last refuge for the Red Squirrel in the south of England.
(Oliver H. Frazer)

It has been said that it all really started in 1789, when the Reverend Gilbert White published his immortal work, *The Natural History and Antiquities of Selborne, in the County of Southampton: with Engravings and an Appendix.* Of course there had been many naturalists, some of considerable distinction, before this time, but none had attained such immediate popular acclaim as he was to experience in the next four years before he died. Although assured of his success, he could not have imagined the full extent of his influence on the study of natural history up to and almost certainly beyond the present day. Originally written in two parts, the first part of the book consisted of a series of letters written to fellow naturalists, mostly describing his own observations on natural history as recorded in his personal diary over a period of some 20 years. The second part comprised a parish history, which, although carefully researched, was never so popular and was omitted from most of the later editions and

reissues, which to date have numbered nearly 300 many with supplementary illustrations and footnotes added. Its secret lay in the magic of its prose, the validity of his first-hand observations and the universal appeal of his chosen subject. He pointed the way along which others could follow in making a concentrated study of the natural history of a small area.

The village of Selborne itself has changed very little over the years and is a place of pilgrimage for dedicated naturalists from all over the world, to visit the church with its memorial window, the ancient yew tree, the little headstone bearing the simple legend "G.W." and the year of his death, 1793, the house and garden at The Wakes where he lived, now the Gilbert White Museum, and then climb up the Zigzag Path to the top of the famous Hanger, with the unforgettable view of the village in the valley below.

With the 200th anniversary of the publication of this remarkable book having been celebrated so recently, it is appropriate to consider the influence it has had in the pursuit of natural history in the Isle of Wight in particular, whilst recalling some of those great naturalists, both amateur and professional, who have helped to reveal and record the Island's treasures, for which the naturalists of today and tomorrow, following in their footsteps, should be eternally grateful.

Like Selborne, the Island is blessed with a very varied landscape embracing a large number of different habitats, each with its own distinctive plants and animals, mainly because of the complexity of the underlying geology and resultant soils. Unlike Selborne, however, the Island has the added advantage of being an island with a varied coastline, providing even more habitats and cliffs in which the geological formations, encapsulating the history of the earth and the development of plant and animal life over a period of 120 million years, are displayed for all to see, and are being constantly renewed by the process of erosion. It is not surprising, therefore, that the geologists were first in the field. At the beginning of the 19th century, however, geology was a very new science and it was a stroke of genius on the part of Sir Henry C. Englefield, Bart., to engage a remarkable Scotsman, Thomas Webster, to carry out a comprehensive survey and to record the results in a series of letters, written between 1811 and 1813, which were to form the second part of a lavishly printed and illustrated guide to the Isle of Wight, published in London in 1816. The letters presented a masterly account of the geological structure of the Island, which was thereafter to be justly regarded as classic ground for geological students. Webster was to become the first Professor of Geology at University College, London, in 1841, but died some three years later. Another geologist, Gideon A. Mantell, enlarged on his work in *Geological Excursions round the Isle of Wight*, published in 1847 and dedicated to H.R.H. Prince Albert, who, with Queen Victoria, had just taken up residence at Osborne House, East Cowes. Many other distinguished geologists, such as Forbes, Bristow and Norman, added to the mounting literature on Isle of Wight geology. In 1857 Professor Richard Owen, later to be the first director of the new Natural History Section of the British Museum at South Kensington, published his monograph on *The Fossil Reptilia of the Wealden Formation*, and incidentally gave us the word 'Dinosaur'. An outstanding amateur at this time, who worked closely with Professor Owen, was the Reverend William Fox, of Brighstone, who, like Gilbert White before him, forsook all chances of preferment and was content to remain a humble curate, surrounded by his beloved fossils. These included bones of two dinosaurs new to science, *Hypsilophodon foxi* and *Polacanthus foxi*, which were named after him. The poet Tennyson, who had come to live at Farringford House, Freshwater, was also most interested in these discoveries, and visited William Fox in company with Professor Owen. Although not a naturalist in the accepted sense, Tennyson was a keen observer of nature and kept in touch with these new developments, and, what is more important, being master of his craft, he was able to express these new ideas in memorable verse. It is fair to say that, with the royal connection at Osborne and Tennyson at Freshwater, the Isle of Wight achieved considerable prominence in these times of scientific investigation and discovery.

With so many visitors to the Island, guide books were in great demand and an important one of these was *The History, Topography, and Antiquities of the Isle of Wight* by W.H. Davenport Adams (1856) in which he expressed his indebtedness to local clergymen, who, with the example of Gilbert White before them, could hardly refuse to combine the study of parish history and the ways of nature with their normal pastoral duties. To meet the growing interest in natural history he included a fourth part containing "a lucid treatise on the Geology of the Island, from the able pen of Ernest P. Wilkins, Esq., of Newport; and a concise essay on its Zoology by a well-known naturalist, the Rev. C.A. Bury, of Sandown." Ernest Wilkins had already established a Museum at Newport and the Rev. Bury, whose notes on zoology were confined to the vertebrates, was already well known as a regular contributor to *The Zoologist*. It makes interesting, but painful, reading; the author and his friends had no concern for conservation and were wont to shoot at anything that moved. There was an element of possessiveness in the amassing of huge collections of stuffed animals and insects in particular, but, in all fairness, it must be accepted that this was a phase in the pursuit of natural history which had to be gone through. There were few, if any, books of reference to help with identification, and specimens had to be obtained and examined closely to provide a detailed description from which future identification could be made.

The wonderful books with clear descriptions and accurate illustrations that we now have to help us in our work have only been made possible by the painstaking study of these early naturalists and their collections. Even then mistakes were made, as characters which happened to be peculiar to one sex only were relied upon. The Rev. Bury had the greatest difficulty in getting the Bank Vole accepted as an Island rodent. We learn, too, that he had difficulty with bats (who doesn't?) and was only able to identify six species, in two of which he was to be proved wrong later. Badgers occurred in a number of places, but had probably "been imported for the amusement of sundry humane and polite inhabitants of the town of Newport, [and] did then and there effect their escape, preferring the retirement of the woods to the notoriety of a public baiting." Otters were also present in several areas and the Pine Marten apparently still inhabited the Undercliff. So far as birds were concerned, the Golden Eagle was seen (and shot) at Appuldurcombe in 1828, the Red-backed Shrike was met with pretty frequently, the Chough, once common, was reduced to a few pairs at Freshwater and Niton, where there were several pairs of Ravens. The list of reptiles and amphibians was as one would expect, but the fish were confined to the few found in fresh water. The only marine vertebrates mentioned were an unidentified Seal, Common Porpoises, a Dolphin (Risso's Grampus) and a stranded Whale (Common Rorqual) whose skeleton is still to be seen at Blackgang Chine. At the end he pays a very touching tribute to his chief informant, Robert Loe, a gamekeeper, born and living all his life in Newchurch. Our native Island naturalist was a fine figure of a man with "a delicacy of feeling and innate refinement that would have graced even the higher walks of society." It seems he died in 1848 from a heart attack brought on by an act of kindness to an aged neighbour.

Davenport Adams published many guides directed at various levels of society, but it was another clergyman, the Rev. Edmund Venables, of Bonchurch, whose *Guide to the Isle of Wight*, published in 1860, now engages our attention. This was a much smaller volume, but what it lacked in the way of lavish illustrations it made up for by a greatly increased section on natural history. He was able to write the section on geology himself by compressing and arranging information contained in what was now a quite extensive range of books on Island geology, but in other departments the field was comparatively untrodden and he had to seek help from his friends, especially the clergy of the Island. Lists of mosses, lichens and fungi were supplied by the Rev. A. Bloxam and the Rev. T. Salwey, but most of the chapters on natural history were the work of an outstanding naturalist of his time, Mr Alexander G. More, FLS, of Bembridge, whose breadth of knowledge was quite remarkable, yet, quite inexplicably, he failed to include the Red Squirrel in his list of mammals. Mr George Guyon contributed information on beetles, and land and freshwater shells, while Miss Elizabeth Kirkpatrick was mainly responsible for the list of seaweeds. With regard to flowering plants, A.G. More was able to draw on the copious information contained in Dr William Arnold Bromfield's *Flora Vectensis*, which had been published in 1856.

Although Mr W.D. Snooke published his *Flora Vectiana* in 1823, it was not intended to be a comprehensive Island flora, but rather an account of some 257 of the rarer and more interesting plants to be found in the Island. When Dr Bromfield, the son of a Hampshire clergyman, came with his sister to live in Ryde in 1836, he was only 35, but had travelled widely in Europe and was an experienced botanist. He soon conceived the idea of preparing a comprehensive flora of the Isle of Wight, and, with Mr Snooke, Dr Bell Salter and other Island botanists, he set about the task of gathering material, This was not going to be a simple list, but each species was to be accompanied by a detailed description of his own making, together with times of flowering and the precise localities where it could be found. In 1843 he discovered the Wood Calamint, *Calamintha sylvatica*, in what is still its only known British station on a chalky bank near Newport. He loved travelling, however, and in the next year he was off to the West Indies, so that work on the flora was suspended. He was nothing if not ambitious, for, on his return, he decided to extend its scope to cover the whole of the county of Hampshire. This was not to be, however, for in 1850, on a visit to the Middle East, he caught a fever in Damascus and on the 9th October, 1851, he died at the age of 50, and the Island lost "a most amiable man and zealous naturalist".

All the work that Mr Snooke been achieved might well have been lost had it not been for his

The Glanville Fritillary at its only remaining breeding site in the south of the Island. (Oliver H. Frazer)

sister, who committed the manuscript, unfinished though it was, to Dr Bell Salter and the famous botanist, Sir William Hooker, of Kew, who acted as editors and filled in the gaps where necessary, so that the long-awaited *Flora Vectensis* was published in 1856. This was to do for the botanists what Thomas Webster's letters had done for the geologists, establishing the Island as classic ground for the study of botany. A.G. More was to continue the work and produced a *Supplement to the Flora Vectensis* in 1872, and another botanist, Frederick Townsend, published the *Flora of Hampshire including the Isle of Wight* in 1884, in which, unfortunately, the Island records tended to be swamped by those from Hampshire. One particularly interesting new plant, however, was Townsend's Cord-grass, *Spartina X townsendii*, named after the author. This was a natural cross between the native *S. maritima* and a recently introduced American species, *S. alterniflora*, first recorded in Southampton Water in 1870 by the brothers H. and J. Groves. It was very strong growing and rapidly spread over the adjacent saltmarshes throughout the Solent area and beyond. In due course, by doubling its chromosome number, a fertile hybrid or new species was formed and named *S. anglica* in 1892, since when it has become the dominant species.

What about the zoologists? How were they progressing? We know that the Rev. Bury had dealt with the vertebrates pretty well, and that A.G. More and others were coming to grips with some of the invertebrates, but there was a long way to go. Strangely enough our own Island speciality, the Glanville Fritillary butterfly, *Melitaea cinxia L.*, was named after Eleanor Glanville, a formidable lady who lived some 100 years before Gilbert White and collected butterflies. She had no connection with the Island, however, as in her day the butterfly in question was found in a number of places. It was first recorded in the Island in 1824, and between 1858 and 1863 it was still locally common on the Kentish coast, but by the turn of the century it had disappeared from all the other known sites and the south coast of the Island became the last stronghold where this butterfly continued to breed, as it still does today.

It was the sheer weight of numbers in the various groups of insects and other invertebrates that made identifying and recording them such a daunting task. It took a lifetime's work by successive dedicated naturalists to produce anything like a representative list. Progress was being made, but the records were dispersed in the pages of numerous journals. An attempt to rectify this was made in the publication of the *Victoria County History for Hampshire and the Isle of Wight* in 1900, containing lists of plants and animals but this suffered from the same defect as Towsend's *Flora*, so far as the Island was concerned. What was wanted was someone in the Island with the necessary ability and drive to gather all these threads together and reveal all the Island's treasures in one volume. Just such a man was waiting in the wings.

His name was Frank Morey, one of the sons of H.W. Morey, the founder of the firm of timber merchants still trading under that name in Newport. Born in 1858, Frank Morey was a dedicated naturalist in the best tradition of Gilbert White. His personal knowledge of the flora and fauna of the Island was immense, and as a member of the Selborne Society and an elected Fellow of the Linnean Society, he was in close touch with most of the best naturalists of the day and was able to enlist their help in gathering material and identifying specimens. Consequently his *Guide to the Natural History of the Isle of Wight*, published in 1909, was far and away the most comprehensive account of the natural history of a well-defined area of considerable size in the country. In its pages he also introduced what at that time were comparatively new branches of natural science, that of seismology, the study of earthquakes, in a short chapter by Professor Milne, who lived at Shide, near Newport, and was a pioneer in this subject, attaining world-wide recognition, especially in Japan, where his name is still revered; and also that of meteorology, the study of weather, with observations and records by John Dover, also a pioneer in this subject, who had established his meteorological station in Totland Bay in 1886, from which he continued to send his records to the Meteorological Office for 61 years without a break.

Frank Morey was the first to realize that the publication of his Guide was only the beginning, and he planned to publish supplementary lists as new records and localities came to light, but the 1914-18 war made this impossible. In 1919, however, he thought of a better way and founded the Isle of Wight Natural History Society, complete with set of rules, list of officers and committee, ready to go into action with himself as Secretary and Editor of *Proceedings*, in which it was proposed to publish supplementary lists annually. They were giants in those days, and the Society got off to a good start. He was a great believer in the importance of education and since 1912, with the aid of his sister, Catherine Morey, had acted as Honorary Curator of the Archaeological Museum at Carisbrooke Castle, which had been opened by Princess Beatrice in 1898 and augmented by suitable antiquities from other collections, including Dr Wilkins' Newport Museum, which had fallen on hard times.

He also undertook to reassemble the fossil specimens derived from this source and other collections to be displayed by agreement in the Sandown Free Library. In 1924 he appointed Mr G.F. Jackson, an eminent geologist from the National Museum of Wales, Cardiff, to be his Scientific Secretary and Curator of what was now to be called the Isle of Wight Museum of Geology, Sandown. Unfortunately he was not to see the complete fulfilment of his plans, as he died at the end of 1925. His sister, Catherine, carried on his work, and in 1935 a new Museum of Natural History at Rylstone Gardens, Shanklin, was opened by Professor Sir Edward Poulton, FRS, of St Helens, with Mr H.F. Poole, of Shanklin, a man of quite exceptional talent, as Honorary Curator. The Island was now served by three specialized museums for the preservation and display of specimens from a single well-defined area, and ambitious plans for improvement were in prospect. These were not to be realized, however, as a stray bomb in 1943 all but destroyed the natural history collections at Shanklin and the other museums suffered from severe neglect. The Society was at a low ebb, but not all was lost.

The full history of the Society has been recorded in *Botany, Birds, Bugs and Barrows on the Isle of Wight* by Leslie Hutchinson, which was published in 1969 on the occasion of the Society's Jubilee. Since then it has gone from strength to strength with a record membership of over 600. Publication of *Proceedings* has been maintained, while a new *Flora of the Isle of Wight*, by Bevis, Kettell and Shepard, was published in 1978. Ornithologists have been well catered for with annual Bird Reports since 1953 by John Stafford, now assisted by an Ornithological Committee. Occasional publications, such as *Watching Birds in the Isle of Wight*, by Jim Cheverton and Bill Shepard, have been produced and more are planned. Attitudes have changed over the years and collecting has given way to conservation. The "Local Look" Countryside Exhibition at Brook during August each year since 1961 has gone a little way to make up for the loss of the Natural History Museum at Shanklin.

The Society has had its ups and downs, but it has remained faithful to the hopes and aspirations of its founder and so, by inference, to Gilbert White. The same cannot be said about many of the elected representatives on our local councils, who have it in their power to determine our future. Over the years they have dismally failed to give the necessary support to any of our efforts. At best they completely ignore our precious heritage, which is our major asset, and at worst they pursue policies which threaten to destroy it and inevitably lead to conflict with those, such as the National Trust, the Nature Conservancy Council and the Society, who are anxious to protect it.

The pursuit of natural history over the last 200 years has been an uphill struggle, rather like climbing the Zigzag Path at Selborne. Now we have reached the top, it would be nice to think that our future was assured, but the mists of ignorance and greed obscure our view of rural harmony that is the charm of Selborne and could be ours. Let us hope that even yet the mists will clear.

The Railways of the Isle of Wight
ALAN DOE

Today, when travelling on the British Rail electric tube trains from Ryde Pier Head to Shanklin it is difficult to think of the railways as being an essential means of transport for the whole Island community. Yet a hundred years ago the choice was between the railway, horse and cart or walking. Although the railways came late to the Island there soon developed a large network of branch lines and even a small town like Ventnor could boast two separate railways reaching it from two different directions.

The first locomotive-hauled line was the Cowes and Newport Railway. Michael Ratsey, a local sailmaker and dignitary, dug the first earth in 1859. The line opened three years later on 16th May 1862, running alongside the River Medina from Cowes to Little London in Newport. Following closely, the Isle of Wight Railway opened a line in 1864 from Ryde St John's Road to Shanklin and on to Ventnor in 1866. This was regarded as the 'main line'; it served the main holiday resorts, carried the most passengers and made the most profit for its shareholders. Ventnor station, at the southern end of the line, was 276 feet above sea level and situated in a large quarry that had been cut into the chalk downland. On leaving the station on a journey to Ryde the train plunged into a long tunnel under St Boniface Down before careering down the relatively steep gradient to Wroxall and Shanklin.

In 1875 the newly formed Ryde and Newport Railway opened its line from Smallbrook Junction (where it branched from the Isle of Wight Railway's line) to Newport, where it joined the Cowes and Newport Railway. At Newport a new station was built next to the old Cowes and Newport Railway's station, for both companies. It had intermediate stations at Ashey, Havenstreet, Wootton and Whippingham. The section from Havenstreet to Wootton now forms the line of the Isle of Wight Steam Railway, a working museum of Island railway history. Neither of these stations is in its original form although Ashey and Whippingham are largely intact. Whippingham station had the distinction of occasionally helping royal visitors on their way to and from the nearby Osborne Estate.

The Isle of Wight (Newport Junction) Railway also opened in 1875. This line meandered through the Vale of Arreton and linked the Isle of Wight Railway's station at Sandown with Newport. Several times the Board of Trade refused permission for sections to open because of the poor standard of construction. The company finally bankrupted itself in its attempt to construct a viaduct for the last mile into Newport station from Pan Lane in 1879, whereupon the line was worked by the Cowes and Newport Railway and the Ryde and Newport Railway, which were being managed jointly. The three companies amalgamated in 1887 to form the Isle of Wight Central Railway with its headquarters at Newport.

Meanwhile, the Isle of Wight Railway had taken over the Brading Harbour Improvement and Railway Company who were responsible for land reclamation and harbour works at the mouth

The Bembridge branch train waits to leave the junction at Brading with locomotive 13 'Carisbrooke' at its head.

(Adrian Searle)

of the River Yar at the eastern end of the Island. From a junction at Brading a delightful line ran via St Helens to Bembridge. For a few years a train ferry carrying wagons operated from St Helens to Langstone harbour on the mainland.

The West Wight was next to be served by a railway. The appropriately named Freshwater, Yarmouth and Newport Railway opened in 1889. Trains were at first provided by the Isle of Wight Central Railway but, following a disagreement in 1913, the company hastily acquired some second hand equipment and itself ran the line from a temporary station adjacent to its larger neighbour. The final line to be opened was from Merstone on the Newport to Sandown line, first to St Lawrence in 1897 and then through to Ventnor via the Undercliff in 1900. The line was noted for its spectacular views over the English Channel after emerging from the St Lawrence tunnel. Ventnor now had two stations, both inconveniently sited high above sea level and away from the town centre.

In 1900 the railway network on the Island boasted 55 miles of track which was owned by five separate railway companies. In addition to the three companies mentioned, two large mainland companies, the London, Brighton and South Coast Railway and the London and South Western Railway, had invested in extending the Isle of Wight Railway's line from Ryde St John's Road northwards to a new pier, by a short tunnel under the Esplanade, at Ryde. Trains could then run along the pier to connect with the Railway-owned ships from Portsmouth.

In the early years of the new century an extraordinary variety of engines, carriages and wagons could be seen on the Island. Most were obtained second hand from the mainland and were well past their best. Despite this, they performed a vital service and their individual charm endeared them to many. The beautifully cleaned red livery of the Beyer Peacock tank engines could be seen working between Ryde and Ventnor. At Newport the motley collection of black liveried engines of the Isle of Wight Central Railway could be seen with the two bright apple green engines of the Freshwater line.

Britain's railways performed heroic tasks during the First World War. Maintenance in those years was neglected and by 1920 the railways of the country were in a poor state. The Railways Act of 1921 amalgamated the dozens of small companies into just four large groups. The Island railways came under the common ownership of the Southern Railway in 1923. Immediate improvements were started. The older engines and carriages were rapidly replaced; tracks and signalling were modernized to accept heavier traffic. Amongst others, the station at Havenstreet was completely rebuilt in 1926. A new railway port at Medina Wharf in Cowes was constructed solely for coal traffic. In this inter-war period the holiday traffic had grown to record levels. The Adams-designed 02 locomotives, brought over from the mainland after 1923, were named after villages and towns. The green livery of the engines was perfectly set off by their brass nameplates with their bright red backgrounds. No 24 'Calbourne' can still be seen at Havenstreet in full working order performing its duties during the summer. In the Thirties, on a summer Saturday, over 36,000 passengers would pass through Ryde Pier and trains would leave the Pier at the rate of one every ten minutes.

However, these scenes of prosperity were not to last as the holiday trade ceased abruptly with the outbreak of war in 1939. During the war the engines, now painted black, worked a much reduced service although there was heavy traffic on the Cowes line as factory workers, engaged on war manufacturing, converged on the town in the morning and left in the evening.

Unlike the railways on the mainland the Island lines did not suffer too badly from the ravages of war. When hostilities ceased it was not long before the gleaming green paintwork appeared again and for a few years tourists flocked to the Island for their holidays. Traffic once again broke all records. A new shade of 'malachite' green paint made the trains look smarter than ever. Just as after the First World War, and for exactly the same reasons, major changes were to come.

In 1948 the railways were nationalized. From that year, by coincidence, it seems as though the railways lost their dominance in the transport of both people and goods. Competition from cars, lorries and buses bit deeper and deeper, and the railway traffic declined alarmingly. On the Island, as elsewhere, the branch lines were the first to feel the full economic effects. In 1952 the Merstone to Ventnor West branch, the last line to open, closed. This was followed closely in 1953 by both the Bembridge and Freshwater branches, thus leaving both the eastern and western extremities of the Island without rail transport. In 1956 a case was made, not without protest, to close the Sandown to Newport line and so railways in the Vale of Arreton were lost forever.

Two lines were left, one from Ryde Pier to

A fine head of steam on the revived Ryde and Newport Railway at Havenstreet.

hand electrified London tube trains. So even now the line retains its distinctive difference from anything on the mainland. The last steam train, or so most people thought, ran from Shanklin to Ryde on 31st December 1966, just 104 years after the first steam journey was made from Cowes to Newport.

The fate of the closed lines has been varied. Many of the stations have become private dwellings and the site of Newport station has disappeared beneath a new relief road and industrial estate. Bembridge station has been replaced by holiday homes and there is a factory on the site of Freshwater station. But in many places the bridges, embankments and cuttings can still be seen clearly from the windows of the buses and cars which caused the railways' downfall.

However, not all was lost. In 1966 a small group of enthusiasts formed the Wight Locomotive Society with the aim of preserving one of the Adams 02 locomotives for static exhibition in Newport. Support was encouraging and the society was not only able to purchase No 24 'Calbourne' but some carriages and wagons as well. The society began to restore the rolling stock at its temporary base at Newport station. Eventually agreement was reached to lease the 1¾ miles of track between Havenstreet and Wootton and on 24th January 1971, just days before scrap men began to take up the track, 'Calbourne' hauled four trains of the society's stock from Newport to its new home. The Isle of Wight Steam Railway was born. Development since 1971 has been rapid. New sidings have been put down, more Island locomotives have been acquired and new workshop and tourist facilities have been built. In 1986 Havenstreet station won the annual national award for being the Best Restored Station in the United Kingdom, a fine tribute to the hard work of the largely volunteer workforce. Future plans include the reconstruction of an all-Victorian train from old carriage bodies made redundant in the 1920s and the exciting prospect of joining up with the British Rail main line at Smallbrook. This 3½ mile extension eastwards from Havenstreet will revive the connection with the old Isle of Wight Railway's Ryde to Ventnor line.

Now, sitting at Havenstreet station on a summer Sunday, it is possible to recreate the days of gleaming green engines and carriages packed to overflowing with holiday-makers. It is reassuring to know that not all of the Island's railway heritage has been lost for ever.

Ventnor, the former Isle of Wight Railway line, the other from Ryde to Cowes, the former Isle of Wight Central line. Newport was no longer a junction or the hub of the Island railway system. By 1960 these lines had become sadly neglected and complete closure was proposed. After considerable protest it was decided that the Cowes to Ryde line would be closed and that the Ryde to Ventnor line would be truncated at Shanklin. Ventnor, once having had two stations, was left without a railway and had to rely on bus transport. The remaining eight miles from Ryde Pier to Shanklin was modernized using second

Quarr Abbey

DENIS BRADLEY

Not far from the ferry terminal at Fishbourne, the Ordnance Survey map indicates two sites for Quarr Abbey, the remains of the medieval abbey in old English lettering, and in modern type its 20th-century neighbour. Indeed, the towers of the new abbey can be seen quite clearly from the car ferry: an intriguing sight for those arriving on the Isle of Wight for the first time. The buildings are also easily visible from the main road between Newport and Ryde, and from the coastal path between Ryde and Wootton. Those whose curiosity is sufficiently aroused to visit the two sites feel, often enough, that they are stepping into another world...

The public bridleway from Binstead runs straight through the scanty remains of the old abbey. Just after the last house of Quarr Road a gate leads into open countryside, and the path heads down into a shallow alley, at the foot of which flows a small stream. Beyond this lies the most conspicuous of the remains: a large building of local stone now used as a barn, but originally storage space for the monastery with part of its sleeping accommodation above. Even this building has been much adapted, and would once have been considerably longer. On the front of it now stands a pretty cottage; it has a rather ecclesiastical appearance for, although not part of the old abbey, it was built in the 18th century using windows and other materials salvaged from the ruins.

Between this building and the stream there is now little to be seen but a rather uneven field, but it is here that the hub of the buildings stood: the cloister, a wide covered passage in the form of a square enclosing a garden, and whose outer walls were formed by the abbey's principal buildings. The barn still standing would have formed the west side of the cloister, and the Abbey Church the south side; but there is now nothing to be seen of the church, and the bridleway runs right over its site. In the middle of the field are a few fragments of the kitchen and refectory walls; beyond are some walls of the abbey's workshops, and further away still the outer wall of the property, fortified against sea-borne raiders.

The present sad condition of the old abbey results from the dissolution of the monasteries in the reign of Henry VIII. Beginning in 1536 with the smaller houses, even the greatest abbeys had been closed by 1540, their goods and lands confiscated, and the monks expelled. For Quarr, which by that time had only ten monks, the end came early, on 22nd July 1536. By the end of September in the same year, much had already been sold: church vessels and ornaments, pictures, furniture, bells, corn and livestock. For a time the church seems to have been maintained as a place of worship, but by 1539 the buildings were being demolished to construct forts at East and West Cowes. Only seventy years later, Sir John Oglander could see no trace of the church, but he did find an old man still living who remembered where it had stood, and said that he had often been inside it. He showed Sir John around what then remained of the other buildings: apparently more extensive than what can be seen today, for they have continued to crumble away over the intervening centuries helped, no doubt, by people in search of free building materials.

In 1544 the estate was bought by John and George Mills; John's grandson sold it in 1609 to Sir Thomas Fleming, the Lord Chief Justice, of whom Sir John Oglander wrote with withering scorn as a parvenu: "So nowe you may see yt greate Abby of Quarr, founded by Baldwin Ryvors, nowe come to ye posteritie of a merchaunt of Nuport. *O tempora, O mores.*"

Sir John even ventured into verse:

That which once ye Abbottes fatte
And sluggische Mounckes did fede,
The druncken Flemminges now doth scrape
With gayne thereof to rayse theyr seed.

He would surely have appreciated the final irony: that in 1912 the descendants of Sir Thomas Fleming sold the ruins to the Benedictine monks of Solesmes.

How have the ruins appeared to later eyes than Sir John's? In 1795 Richard Warner comments succinctly in his *History of the Isle of*

Outside Dom Paul Belliot's masterpiece ... the 20th-century version of Quarr Abbey.

Wight: 'The situation of this religious house is a very pleasing and secluded one; commanding a charming view of the water, and deeply embosomed in woods".

Later, in 1864, W.H. Davenport Adams abandons himself to a more romanticized view in his *History and Topography:* 'The deathless ivy clambers over the few hoary stones that remain to tell us of the skill of its Norman architects. A broad, green meadow blooms, where once stood the cells and chambers of the pious monks... The refectory, where once the good monks did justice to their good cheer, is now a barn... One should visit this 'hallowed ground', as Scott would have one visit Melrose, 'by the pale moonlight', when the far-off waters play in the track of the tremulous glory, and a certain holiness of feeling seems to surround the mossy ruin. Again, as one muses in the silence, the past grows into life and action. One hears the vespers chiming through the young green elms... The cowled monks move

noiselessly through the stilly glades..."

It is, though, true even today, and despite the inevitable intrusions of the 20th century, that the site remains a place where it is easy to feel at peace, and where many are bound to wonder who these monks were, and how they lived their daily lives.

In the early fourth century, when Christians were no longer being persecuted, and the faithful no longer had to be prepared to make the supreme sacrifice for the sake of their religion, a movement began among some who wished nevertheless to devote their whole lives to their Creator. Men and women would leave their homes, and go into the Egyptian desert to live as hermits, alone with God, and for God alone. Holy men who had lived in the desert for many years would naturally be sought out by newcomers, anxious to learn from their wisdom how best to embark upon the solitary life, so full of pitfalls for the inexperienced. Some of these wise men would attract large numbers of followers, and in the course of time the first monastic communities developed from such groups, as they became structured and permanent, and acquired a 'Rule' or Code of Life composed by the *Abba*, the Father of the community.

One such *Abba*, or 'Abbot', came to outshine all the others in importance, not only because he lived in Italy instead of in Egypt, and so was able to adapt the monastic life to European conditions, but also because the Rule he composed was so manifestly balanced and practical. This was St Benedict, who lived from c.480 to c.540. His Rule quickly spread to most parts of Europe, and has been the basis of western monasticism ever since.

In the course of its history the Rule of St Benedict has been adapted successfully to many different times and cultures - a sign of St Benedict's breadth of vision - and there have also been reform movements seeking to return to a more literal observance of the Rule. On the eve of the foundation of Quarr, two important centres of such a reform were established across the Channel: Cîteaux in 1098, and Savigny in 1105. It was from Savigny that Quarr was founded in 1132, but soon after, in 1147, Savigny and its daughter houses were admitted to the order of Cîteaux. Quarr was therefore a Cistercian abbey for most of its history.

Since the Cistercians had turned away from the adaptations and relaxations of the Rule that had become customary in the course of the centuries, their daily life, particularly in the early years of the reform, was one of considerable austerity. Silence was strictly observed, so that, although speech could always be used at the proper times for the giving of instruction and for conversation on spiritual matters, the monks would have had no opportunity for casual talk; even for necessary communication about their daily life and work a system of sign language was used so that words might be avoided.

The diet, too, was austere. Following the Rule, the Cistercians abstained totally from meat, its use being permitted only to the sick brethren in the infirmary (although there was a growing tendency to grant admission to the infirmary quite liberally). Fish also was not at first a normal part of the monastic diet, and was reserved for special treats (known as 'pittances') on feast days or in memory of some benefactor. During Lent not even butter, cheese or eggs were allowed; only bread and vegetables. The normal drink was wine, beer or cider, depending on the locality, in seemingly generous quantities (up to about two pints a day), but it must be remembered that safe drinking water to supplement this was not generally available.

Austerity was also the hallmark of the Cistercian liturgy, and whereas the monks would spend between four and five hours each day at the various services - the night office, the Mass, and the seven offices that punctuated the daylight hours - this was a very considerable reduction on the amount of time the mainstream Benedictines of the period devoted to worship. Ceremonial and music were also drastically simplified, and church furnishings and ornamentation were kept plain.

The monks' day, as envisaged by St Benedict, was always arranged around the one night office and seven day-time offices already mentioned, but the times of these offices were fixed, not by clocks, but by the sun; thus the interval between the daybreak office of Lauds and the nightfall office of Compline was much longer in summer than in winter, and this allowed more time to be spent in manual labour in the fields at the season when there was most farm work to be done. The Cistercians, who took their monasteries back to the countryside and became farmers on a large scale, also returned to St Benedict's timetable. Throughout the year they rose soon after midnight for the night office and did not return to their beds afterwards, instead using the remaining hours of darkness for reading and meditation. Manual work occupied about six hours a day in summer, and about two hours in winter. The monks were allowed about eight hours sleep, but in summer, when the nights were so short, they would have to make up the balance with a siesta at about noon.

One further feature of Cistercian life must be mentioned, because it is of the greatest importance. This is that in each monastery there were two almost distinct communities: the choir monks, who followed the régime just described; and the lay brothers (known as *conversi*) who lived in separate quarters, had a different and less demanding form of worship, and spent long hours in manual work. In the Cistercian system, abbeys usually operated several outlying farms, called 'granges', which would be staffed by small groups of lay brothers, who returned to the abbey only on Sundays and the greater feasts.

This institution of the lay brotherhood both ensured the viability of the abbey's economy, and provided a form of religious life suitable for the simple and uneducated.

Quarr Abbey was founded in 1132 by Baldwin de Redvers, Earl of Devon and later Lord of the Isle of Wight, and survived until 1536. The painstaking researches of the late Dom Frederick Hockey assembled a large amount of material, mainly in the form of legal documents and account rolls, used as the basis of his masterly study *Quarr Abbey and its lands: 1132-1631.* Unfortunately there remain whole areas about which almost nothing is known; and while it is certain that the lives of the monks would have conformed to the Cistercian pattern already described, scarcely any personal information about them has come to light.

Even the size of the community can scarcely be guessed, but the fact that the surviving ruins all seem to date from the mid-13th century appears to show that the original plan was outgrown during the first hundred years. A healthy level of recruitment is also indicated by the ability. of Quarr to make two foundations: Stanley Abbey in Wiltshire in 1154, and Buckland in Devonshire in 1278. The Buckland foundation was made in fact at a time when the Cistercian population in most places was falling sharply, and few abbeys were in a position to contemplate expansion; Quarr would thus seem to have been among the more vigorous communities at this stage.

Like almost all Cistercian houses, Quarr had its network of granges, most of them on the Island, and including such familiar names as Combley, Staplers, Heasley, Luccombe and Hamstead. The 'home grange' of Newnham was less than a mile from the abbey, and it is quite possible that Arreton, though in theory a manor, was also worked as a grange. During the 12th and early 13th centuries it is likely, to judge from the situation elsewhere, that the lay brothers, who looked after the granges and did much of the building and craft work at the abbey itself, outnumbered the choir monks. But things began to change everywhere in the course of the 13th century. For various reasons the number of lay brothers began to decline; inevitably the grange system could no longer be maintained, the farms had to be leased to tenants, and Quarr, like other houses, became dependent on rents instead of farming for its livelihood.

Some abbeys seem to have fared relatively well in this new situation—Quarr's own daughter house Stanley was counted among the greater abbeys at the time of the dissolution—but Quarr faced additional problems: the Hundred Years War of 1337-1453 hit the Solent coasts particularly hard, and the abbey's economy must have been seriously damaged by the need to provide for the fortification and defence of the coast, as well as by the general devastation of the northern part of the Island in 1377 by invading French troops. On the other hand, there are indications that recruitment remained steady if not spectacular; it is also possible that some of the younger monks may have been discharged in the year preceding the dissolution, and so were not included in the final total—but this can only be conjecture. Whatever the case, the situation recorded by the King's commissioners makes a sad conclusion for an abbey that could once have housed a hundred or more monks, and which enjoyed a good reputation right up to the end: ten monks, 39 employees and a very modest income.

The Cistercians had lived at Quarr for more than 400 years. They were expelled, and their buildings fell into ruin... but before another 400 years had passed monks had returned to Quarr: from the viewpoint at the top of the bridleway from Binstead the towers of the new abbey seem almost to be rising out of the ruins of the old.

The new buildings are certainly striking, even exotic. Constructed entirely in specially imported Flemish brick, its warm natural colours ranging from deep rose to pale yellow, the ground plan of the monastery is quite traditional, with the principal buildings ranged around a cloister garden as in the old abbey. The style, however, is most original, Moorish elements intertwining with many other influences to give buildings both rich and simple, austere and homely. It is one of the earliest, and perhaps the best of all the remarkable works of Paul Bellot, who had qualified as an architect before becoming a member of the French monastic community that was to make its home at Quarr in 1908.

This time the monks were not Cistercians but Benedictines, the famous abbey of Solesmes in exile. The French Revolution (1789) had brought all monastic life in France to an end, but in the 1830s the deserted Benedictine priory of Solesmes, near Le Mans, was revived by a young priest, Dom Prosper Guéranger. The early years were difficult; but eventually growth became rapid, and by 1901 Solesmes stood at the head of a congregation of some ten autonomous abbeys and priories (its own daughter and 'grand-daughter' houses), while itself remaining a large community of 90 monks. The congregation also included by now three communities of nuns.

In 1901, however, a serious problem arose. Since the Revolution, religious orders had had no legal existence in France. Now the government sought to rectify this: all associations were required to seek official registration, or face closure and confiscation of their assets. Recognizing the sinister anti-clerical motivation behind this ostensibly liberal piece of legislation, the Benedictine communities decided unanimously at the end of April not to comply, and therefore had no choice but to go into exile. Events were to prove this difficult decision the right one.

With 1st October as the deadline for compliance with the new law, it was necessary to act quickly. Early in July the Abbot of Solesmes, Dom Paul Delatte, sent one of his officials, Dom Maurice Noetinger, to England, which Dom Guéranger himself had thought of as a possible place of refuge in case of persecution, and where a monastery of the congregation, at Farnborough, had existed since 1895. At the beginning of August Dom Noetinger reported that he had found a house that would do. This was Appuldurcombe House near Wroxall on the Isle of Wight.

Appuldurcombe had at that time been standing empty for 18 months, and the small advance guard of monks had a full month's hard work cleaning the house, and erecting partitions to divide large rooms into enough monastic cells for their brethren. By 21st September the whole community had arrived, some having crossed from St Malo, and the remainder from Le Havre. It is said that some of the more elderly monks had never caught sight of the sea before, and were as excited as children to see what enormous ships it was able to support.

Conditions in the house were cramped but tolerable. At first the community had imagined their exile lasting only a few months; but when it became clear, as it soon did, that they would have to stay much longer they decided on the construction of a temporary church. For a building of timber and corrugated iron it was quite attractive; it both relieved some of the congestion inside the house, and allowed the monks to celebrate the liturgy with something of the splendour they had been accustomed to at Solesmes.

Exiles from a country where, at that time, everything possible was done to make life difficult for members of religious orders, the monks were amazed by the hospitality offered them in England: "a land of true freedom", wrote Abbot Delatte, adding that English law and customs give shelter to all who settle their debts, pay their taxes, and do not have brushes with the police or disturb the peace at night! Among the local inhabitants they aroused understandable curiosity, and they were quietly amused at the furtive glances to see whether Papists really had cloven hoofs, and at the small boys on whose lips the word "monk" somehow became "monkey" when they thought they were out of earshot; very quickly, however, they were completely accepted and welcomed as good, if somewhat eccentric, neighbours.

In 1907 there was a fresh problem: the monks would have to leave Appuldurcombe the following year, and were unable to return to France. The solution adopted was to purchase Quarr Abbey House and to build on to it the essentials of a monastery (the house itself being far too small); the temporary church would be transported from Appuldurcombe until a permanent one could be envisaged.

Quarr Abbey House had been built by Admiral Sir Thomas Cochrane on land purchased from the Fleming family in 1858. With Osborne House so close, this was then a fashionable area. Sir Thomas's daughter, Minna, was lady-in-waiting to Princess Beatrice, and Queen Victoria herself is said to have been a frequent visitor to Quarr.

When the monks bought the house in May 1907 it had been standing empty for some years. Once again it was a race against time, since Appuldurcombe had to be evacuated the following summer. The architect, Dom Paul Bellot, took up residence at Quarr and directed the building operations personally, even instructing the bricklayers in the technique of building arches. By mid-July 1908, in record time, everything was finished and the Community installed, thanks to the hard work of about 280 local men employed on the construction. As a way of showing his gratitude for their dedication, the Abbot of Solesmes entertained them all to dinner in Ryde Town Hall on 29th February 1908. Later, the buildings were completed in two further phases: the church was built between 1911 and

1912, a masterpiece by any standards; and finally the temporary church was removed to be replaced by the guesthouse, porter's lodge and main entrance, to form the fourth side of the cloister.

The end of the First World War brought a change in the situation: it was now possible for the monks to return to France, but should they do so, and what would then become of Quarr? After much heart searching, for the years on the Island had been very happy ones, it was decided to leave behind a substantial group of about 25 monks, while the rest of the community returned home in 1922. In due course the arrival of novices showed that Quarr could eventually grow into an English-speaking community... and this is what happened. In 1937 – still in majority French – it became an autonomous abbey under Abbot Gabriel Tissot; and in 1964, on Abbot Tissot's retirement, the present Abbot, Dom Aelred Sillem, an Englishman, was elected. Quarr has for many years now been fully at home in England, no longer a "little French island" as the exiles could not help being. On the other hand, it has retained all its links with Solesmes, its mother house, and with its 'cousins', the monasteries of the Solesmes Congregation in France and several other countries. Quarr thus seeks in a quiet way to transcend national and cultural boundaries.

The monks of Solesmes were not, however, the first contemplative religious to arrive on the Island: Dominican nuns had been established in their priory overlooking Carisbrooke Castle since 1866, and a community of Benedictine nuns from Belgium had opened a convent and a small school at Steephill in 1882.

Nor were the monks the only refugees to come to the Island in the first years of the century: two communities of French Benedictine nuns arrived at about the same time. The 37 nuns of the abbey of Saint Michel in Brittany made their temporary home at Clarence House, near Osborne; while the nuns of Sainte Cécile de Solesmes went first to Northwood House, and then, in 1906, to Ryde, where they added a church and other monastic buildings to Appley House to form what is now known as St Cecilia's Abbey.

Both these communities returned to France after the First World War, but the buildings at Ryde were not left empty: they were taken over by the nuns of Steephill who had for some time been looking for a more suitable home for themselves and their school. In these new surroundings, the community's way of life came to resemble more and more that of the Solesmes nuns who had preceded them. The school was first reduced in size, and then, in 1939, closed completely; and at last, in 1950, St Cecilia's Abbey was admitted to full membership of the Congregation of Solesmes. Today it is a thriving community with an international membership.

These two communities – the monks and the nuns – base their life on St Benedict's Rule interpreted in as straightforward a manner as possible, not attempting to emulate the austerities of the medieval Cistercians, but nevertheless safeguarding a certain simplicity, even frugality, in regard to material things. The day, although now regulated by the clock rather than by the sun, is one that St Benedict and the Cistercians would surely recognize as their own: a balance of prayer, reading and study, and manual work arranged within the framework of the various offices in church. The music used at these offices is the ancient Gregorian Chant, much of which dates back to the 8th century or earlier. It is in very great measure thanks to the persevering researches undertaken by the monks of Solesmes over more than a century that the chant has been restored from the debased form it had taken by the early 19th century to its original beauty; and the Island can take pride in the fact that some of the most fruitful years for this research were those spent at Appuldurcombe and Quarr. In recent years the nuns of St Cecilia's have become known internationally for their recordings of this hauntingly beautiful and prayerful music.

This is not the place to discuss the deeper motivation of such a life. It could perhaps have been called an anachronism in any century, and maybe after all the word is an appropriate one; for as monks and nuns live to some extent withdrawn from the world in the seclusion of the monastic enclosure, but by doing so in no way reject the world, so in a sense they withdraw from their own time, but not by any means rejecting it, in order to see it, and to lead their lives, in the context of eternity.